Communicating About Differences

Understanding, Appreciating, and Talking about Our Divergent Points of View

SECOND EDITION

Carl Welte

Copyright © 2022 Carl Welte.

All rights reserved. No part of this book may be reproduced, stored, or transmitted by any means—whether auditory, graphic, mechanical, or electronic—without written permission of both publisher and author, except in the case of brief excerpts used in critical articles and reviews. Unauthorized reproduction of any part of this work is illegal and is punishable by law.

ISBN: 979-8-88640-250-6 (sc)
ISBN: 979-8-88640-251-3 (hc)
ISBN: 979-8-88640-252-0 (e)

Because of the dynamic nature of the Internet, any web addresses or links contained in this book may have changed since publication and may no longer be valid. The views expressed in this work are solely those of the author and do not necessarily reflect the views of the publisher, and the publisher hereby disclaims any responsibility for them.

One Galleria Blvd., Suite 1900, Metairie, LA 70001
1-888-421-2397

Also by Carl Welte

*Making and Fulfilling Your Dreams as a Leader:
A Practical Guide for Formulating and Executing Strategy*

*Building Commitment:
Unleashing the Human Potential at Work*

To my dear friend Dr. William H. Pemberton, Ph.D. Bill helped me appreciate the importance of being me, and continually work at becoming a better me.

Bill was a cherished mentor, teacher and friend. We shared many meaningful experiences in his office, over a meal, or in various classroom teaching experiences around the country. I miss him deeply.

Bill was a consulting psychologist with a private practice in Mill Valley, California.

CONTENTS

Preface to the Second Edition ix
Introduction xi

1. The Communication Process: Understanding the Basics 1
2. Perception: The Map Is Not the Territory 14
3. The Structure of Magic:
   Skillfully Communicating about Differences 43

Appendix A: Answers and Comments 75
Appendix B: Putting It to Work:
           Crafting Improvement Strategies 85
Endnotes 95
About the Author 99

PREFACE TO THE SECOND EDITION

This new and improved edition of *Communicating about Differences* contains enhancements to provide greater clarity to enable the reader to understand and apply the important concepts, structures, practices, processes and tools provided. A greater understanding that allows for increased awareness of self and others, and to use skillful communication patterns to seek to understand and be understood.

INTRODUCTION

Differences between people are inevitable. Sometimes these differences evolve into serious conflict. Often times these differences drag on or go unresolved leaving battle scars. These differences occur because the world shows up differently for each of us leading to individual interpretations as to what is going on. And it is important to be able to skillfully communicate about such differences.

We will explore the structure of our divergent interpretations as to what is going on. An understanding and appreciation of the roots of our divergent points of view is important. And it is critical to realize that what is going on and one's perception of what is going are two different things. This distinction is necessary to allow for genuine communication about our differences. The purpose of communicating about differences is not necessarily to agree, but to come to a mutual understanding of our divergent points of view. And perhaps to move things to a new and better place.

The purpose of this book is to enhance your level of consciousness regarding the dynamics of differences when they occur and to increase your level of confidence and competence in communicating about such differences

To serve as a useful guide I wanted this book to be brief and straight forward, while at the same time really saying something. I also wanted to have you become actively engaged in the process. Toward this end, exercises are included along the way to enhance your understanding of the material. Also, a section is included to provide some coaching to help you work on anything thing you might want to work on regarding your communications effectiveness.

This book is for anyone who wants to develop a keener awareness of self and others; and, to use such awareness to enhance communications and relationships by using effective communication patterns. But leaders will find it especially valuable.

Communicating about Differences complements my two books written for organizational leaders. These two books equip leaders with the clarity, confidence, and competence to effectively address the two strategic imperatives for growing and sustaining a successfully organization. The first imperative is to develop and implement a *sound strategy*. The second imperative is to grow and sustain a *culture of commitment* that energizes people to struggle to achieve the sound strategy.

My book, *Making and Fulfilling Your Dreams as a Leader: A Practical Guide for Formulating and Executing Strategy*[1] addresses the first imperative. Its purpose is to enable the leader to formulate and execute a *sound strategy*. A practical and proven strategic framework is proved to enable the leader to develop and live a sound strategy on an ongoing basis to propel the organization forward.

My book, *Building Commitment: Unleashing the Human Potential at Work*[2] addresses the second imperative. Its purpose is to enable the leader to build and sustain a work culture of commitment to achieve the sound strategy.

Leaders will find *Communicating about Differences* to be especially valuable in helping them achieve these two strategic imperatives. To be effective, they need to establish credibility, the foundation of leadership. This book helps them establish such credibility by helping them increase their awareness of self and others; and, to master the requisite skillful communication patterns to complement such awareness. These capabilities are of paramount importance in being an effective leader, especially in dealing with difficult situations. And dealing with difficult situations, and having tough conversations relative to such situations, are an integral part of being an effective leader.

Let us lay the groundwork for the book.

The purpose of a well-intentioned sender and receiver in the communication process is to seek to understand, be understood, or both. The phrase "a well-intentioned sender and receiver" is used because many times a party or parties engaged in talking do not care to be understood or try to understand. The sender perhaps just wants to talk, or maybe is just blowing off steam. And perhaps the receiver does not care about wasting energy to explore the topic, or is really not that interested about what the receiver has to say. And when it comes to politics, obfuscation rather than transparency or clarity often prevails.

This book is written to help you be more effective in communicating when it is important for you to understand or be understood. Those times when you need to go beyond the surface level and go into a deeper level to uncover or express the true meaning, feeling, or motive. And especially those times when there are obvious or uncovered different points of view, be they small or large.

The first chapter, *The Communications Process: Understanding the Basics* may be a little bit understated. The chapter lays out the basic elements involved in the communications process. But it does more than that by discussing some aspects of communication that you may not have realized, and that can be extremely valuable to you.

The second chapter, *Perception: The Map Is Not the Territory*, provides valuable concepts, structures, and exercises to take you to a deeper level of realization and appreciation of the fact that everyone has their own unique windows of the world. Such an understanding and appreciation provides you with a solid foundation for engaging in skillful communication, the subject of the next chapter.

The third chapter, *The Structure of Magic: Skillfully Communicating about Differences*, takes you through a practical and proven structure of effective listening and speaking patterns to enable you to increase your effectiveness in seeking to understand and be understood.

Appendix A, *Exercise Answers and Comments,* allows you to check the work you have done on the various exercises throughout the book that are designed to enhance your learning experience.

Appendix B, *Putting It to Work: Crafting Improvement Strategies*, helps you put the concepts, structures, and tools discussed in the book to use in becoming a more skillful communicator, especially in difficult situations. It provides you with a practical and proven process for crafting specific improvement strategies for things you may want to work on.

1. THE COMMUNICATION PROCESS: UNDERSTANDING THE BASICS

The purpose of communication is to achieve shared understanding.

Talking is not communicating; and hearing is not listening.

While on the surface the communications process would seem to be rather straight forward, there is actually a lot going on, as illustrated in Figure 1.1.

Figure 1.1: The Communications Process

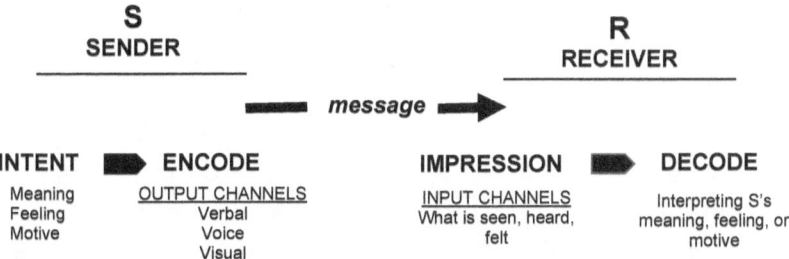

Let's briefly discuss the primary components of the communication process.

Intent

This is what you want to communicate. Your meaning, feeling, or motive, or all three.

Encode

You encode your messages by using the output channels, the three Vs – verbal, voice, and visual. They can each be described as follows:

Verbal: The words. The content of the message.
Voice: The tone, tempo, inflections.
Visual: Body language, expressions, gestures.

The voice and visual are commonly referred to as the nonverbals.

Impression

You initially receive messages via your input channels. What you see, hear, or feel. The impression is a fundamental activity between your nerve endings and what is going on. But even at this basic level differences arise. And you will perceive things differently from one instance to the next.

Decode

You decode the message by moving from what the sender says or does to your interpretation or translation of what the sender says or does. In simple conversation they may be one in the same. But when the two are not in sync for you, and it is important to you or to the sender that you understand, you may need to enter into conversation to gain clarity. And the work you may need to do to clear things up becomes a little or a lot more difficult when there are apparent or real differences between you and who you are attempting to communicate with.

With a comprehensive knowledge of the communication process in tow, let us now discuss some important points for you to be aware of as a sender and receiver.

You as Sender

- It is important to *tailor your message* to your target audience, be it an individual or group. The more you know your audience the more you are in a position to communicate in a way that aligns with their interest, knowledge, and feelings regarding the subject of your communication.

- You need to *pace with your audience* by speeding up or slowing down the speed of your delivery. You want to continually do so by being observant of your receiver and his degree of attention. If he is with you, get on with it. But if he does not appear to be with you, you many need to slow down, test for interest or understanding by asking questions, or just shut up or change the subject.

    Relating to pacing, it is not only interesting but important to realize that there are significant *physiological differences* between the sender's ability to speak the words and the receiver's physical ability to hear the words. In general, the receiver can hear four times faster than the speaker. With his rudimentary voice box to get the words out, in general the speaker can go at a rate of 100–150 words per minute; whereas the receiver can hear at a rate of 450-600 words per minute.

    An important caveat here. When talking, if you require your receiver to cycle back into his memory bank to call up something that relates to what you are communicating, be aware that this 4:1 ratio can quickly change. All of a sudden you may leap ahead of your receiver. So be cognizant of your message and what you are requiring the receiver to do. And again, always be observant of your receiver to ascertain whether rather or not she is pacing with you.

- To your receiver, your *nonverbal communications (voice and visuals) are a powerful* component of your message. This is especially true when you are worked up about your message. So be aware of your nonverbals and amplify or diminish them to align with the message you want to deliver. If you want to emphasize your message in general, or a particular aspect, perhaps raise your voice, or get more animated. By contrast, tone things down or become more still if called for. Your basic nature of course will have a lot to do with your tendency to amplify or diminish your messages.

As powerful as the nonverbals may be to the interpretation of a message, over the years there has been misinformation floating around the academic environment and beyond greatly overstating the potency of the voice and visual output channels to the receiver. The claim has been that the meaning of the message is 7 percent verbal, 38 percent vocal and 55 percent visual, meaning that 97% of the meaning of the message is nonverbal. This "7-55-38 formula" as it became to be known stemmed from research done in the 1960s by Albert Mehrabian and colleagues at the University of California at Los Angeles. This formula has since been debunked. The research had limitations and the research team has stated that their research was misunderstood. But the formula did get legs and you need to be aware of it just in case you have heard of it or come across it.[1]

But if we just think about it, most of the messages we send or receive are straight forward and reliant mainly on the words spoken and received. The formula however does gain credence when we amp up the emotions on the part of either the sender or the receiver in a communications effort.

- It is important to *use the appropriate communication medium* when communicating your message. Think about the relationship between the output channels and the communication mediums you most commonly use as illustrated below:

Figure 1.2: Communication Mediums and Output Channels

Communications medium	Output channels involved
letter, fax, email, social media	Verbal
telephone, voicemail	Verbal + Voice
face-to-face, video conferencing, social media with video included	Verbal + Voice + Visual

The take away here is to use the appropriate communications medium that best fits your message, your audience, and the time required by the various mediums to formulate and deliver your message.

In so doing, you want to weigh the content of your message, your level of rapport with your audience, and the audience's knowledge of your subject. The more complex your subject, the more you want to use a communications medium that involves more than just the verbal. And the greater the rapport you have with your audience and their knowledge of your subject, the less you have to worry about the communication medium used.

This all seems so basic. And it is. But you know of people and cases where the communication mediums are over used, under used, or used inappropriately. For example, overusing email, including using it to transmit information that should be done in person.

And of course, there are instances that you will want to use a combination of mediums. For example, summarizing the results of a face-to-face meeting with some appropriate documentation.

- In *communicating important messages*:

    - *Embellish the content* of your message by *using appropriate examples* to clarify key points.
    - *Display appropriate emotion* to add your feelings to your meaning by making use of: a) your voice output channel through varying the tone of your voice, the speed of delivery and pausing; and, b) your visual output channel through using gestures and perhaps moving around.
    - In addition to using examples, *use symbolic language*[2] such as metaphors and stories to clarify key points.

- Most people have a preference in how they use the three senses of seeing, hearing, and feeling to take in (receive) and transmit (send) information. We all use all three senses, but most people have a preference. To some people this preference is quite pronounced. The other two senses, smelling and tasting, do not play much of a role in communications unless those senses are called for to assess a task at hand, such as tasting a food item. Bandler and Grinder called this preference for favoring one of the three senses the *representational system*. They referred to the three senses as *visual* (seeing), *auditory* (hearing), and *kinesthetic* (feeling)[3]. A person with a kinesthetic preference values experiencing things.

With people you interact with on a frequent basis you should be able to pick out these preferences if indeed they do exist. Tune into the kinds of words people use on a consistent basis.

For example:

- *"I see your point."*
  "But that is only my view."
  (Visual)

- *"Sounds good to me."*
  "At least that's what I hear."
  (Auditory)

- *"I think I have a good feel for what you are trying to say."*
  "My experience has always been that…"
  (Kinesthetic)

In serious conversation, the value of knowing one's preferred representational system allows you to align with your receiver's preferred system when speaking to enhance rapport and gain clarity.

When addressing a group in making important announcements or in training experiences you want to attempt to incorporate all three representational systems into your communications. You can do so by perhaps reinforcing the words with handouts, using visual aids, and involving your audience by having them do something.

- In like manner, most people have preferred natural thinking and behavioral preferences or styles. Most times, because they are a natural part of a person, such preferences occur at a subconscious level.

Even though you may not be familiar with the two individual assessment instruments briefly described below, they are helpful in understanding the nature of these preferences.

The *Myers-Briggs Type Indicator* focuses on character and temperament.

Its structure consists of four pairs of preferences:

> *Extraversion vs. Introversion*
> *Intuition vs. Sensation (the facts)*
> *Thinking vs. Feeling*
> *Judging (closure) vs. Perceiving (open options)*

The *DISC* assessment focuses on behavioral style. It's four styles are:

	Behavioral Style	Description/Preferences
D	Dominance	Driver; results; assertive; action; bottom line; control; independence; decisive.
I	Influencing	Relationships; people; persuasive; seeks approval; dislikes structure.
S	Steadiness	Progress; collaboration; stability; teamwork; harmony; staying the course.
C	Conscientiousness	Security; stability; proven; thorough; facts; assurance; patient; standards.

Although I am not promoting these two popular assessments, they are good at what they deliver for the general population*. There are

---

* If you are interested in learning more about either of these two assessments discussed above refer to the Endnotes at the back of the book for Chapter One, footnote 4.

other assessments, for example leadership, organizational, sales and learning assessments, that are designed for specific audiences or purposes.

Although such models can be very useful, such frameworks are not mandatory for you to better understand the thinking and behavioral preferences of people you interact with on a frequent basis. Just pay attention.

The value once again of identifying such preferences is that in important conversations you can gain greater rapport and be more effective, no matter what your natural thinking and behavioral preferences are, *by adapting to the thinking and behavioral preferences* of whomever you are interacting with. Think of yourself as a rubber band stretching out to meet the person you are interacting with.

Stereotype Mode

Based on his research, Glen Strasburg, Professor-Emeritus the University of California, Los Angeles and California State University, East Bay posits that most people use definite verbal, voice, or visual patterns to signal when they have had enough of the conversation and want to bale. What happens, he describes, is that the crispness of one's perception diminishes as they experience accumulative units of stress or boredom. That makes sense. But what is interesting is that rather than slowly continuing on a downward trajectory, the bottom falls out all of sudden and the person so indicates by exhibiting what is for them a stereotype mode by using a personal pattern of verbal, voice, or visual signals.

Figure 1.3: Stereotype Mode

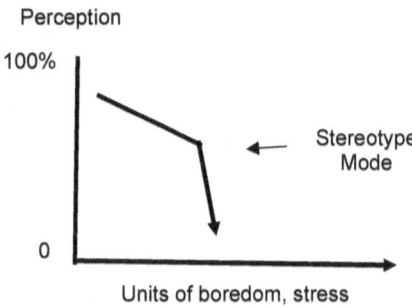

For most people, if indeed they have a stereotype mode, they are unaware of it. When I first became aware of this phenomenon, I asked my staff for some feedback. It was an office setting. They said that I displayed such a mode when I had enough. And what I did is turn to my right and fiddle with papers on my desk.

So what value was such feedback to me? It was very valuable. Because when I felt myself slipping into my stereotype mode, I could course correct and get reengaged. That, of course, is assuming I wanted to. And if I did not want to get reengaged, the better alternative was is to express that I had enough.

Do you know your stereotype mode? If not, are interested in discovering it?

If so, work with an adult friend or friends. Adult friends are better sources of feedback than family members. Family members will most likely be hesitant to provide you with honest feedback because they are too close to you and fearful of harming the relationship. Explain the stereotype mode to an adult friend and ask for their feedback. Then thank them.

You as Receiver

There is a lot to say about you as a receiver, but that is saved for Chapter 2 which focuses on perception, and Chapter 3 which focuses on effective communication patterns in communicating about differences.

But this is a good time to talk about levels of listening.

Figure 1.3: Levels of Listening

1. **Ignore**
   - Non-listening; tune out, consciously or unconsciously.
   - The message: *"I don't care"* or *"You're not important."*

2. **Passive Listening**
   - Very common.
   - To many listening means "be there and be quiet".
   - Often frustrating because of lack of feedback.

3. **Selective Listening**
   - Listen to what we want to listen to.
   - When one determines to be interested, may function at Level 4 (Attentive Listening) or Level 5 (Active Listening). When one determines not to be interested, may function at Level 2 (Passive Listening) or Level 1 (Non-Listening).
   - The problem at this level is that as listeners we are inconsistent and judgmental.

4. **Attentive Listening**
   Tuned in, interested, and participating. But the focus is only on the content or facts of the message and not the emotion. At this level can tell you what you said, but not necessarily what you meant.

5. **Active Listening**
   Listen in a manner that shows care and respect. Seek to understand the total message, that is, meaning, feeling, and motive, by participating and demonstrating understanding.

Active listening is thoroughly covered in Chapter 3. This is the type of listening you want to do when the speaker really wants you to understand, you really want to understand, or you both want to assure shared understanding occurs.

As effective and essential as it is in attempting to achieve understanding, you will not want to be an active listener on a continuous basis. For one thing, you will be a big bore and people will avoid you. For another, active listening is hard work and can be exhausting. You need to concentrate and track with the speaker, demonstrate that you are seeking to understand, and check out your understanding through inquiry, paraphrasing/ speculating about the speaker's real meaning, feeling, and motive. That's a lot. So, you need to pick your spots. The topic and the needs of the sender and yourself will determine when that is. And with good active listening skills it will become easier and certainly be worth it.

Communication Barriers

Exercise 1.1: Identifying Communication Barriers

Purpose

Heighten your awareness of all the things that get in the way of achieving understanding in the communication process. And with a greater awareness be able to minimize your creation of such obstacles.

<u>What to Do</u>

1. Take a few moments, and on a sheet of paper jot down verbal, vocal, and visual behaviors that can get in the way of communications between a sender and receiver.

2. Compare your list with the list in Appendix A, "Answers and Comments", **Exercise 1.1: Communication Barriers**, page 75

There are no right or wrong answers. Nor is the intent to have either of the two lists be exhaustive. The intent is to raise your awareness a bit so you will be better prepared to avoid creating such barriers and to self-correct when you catch yourself engaging in such behaviors.

Where We Are

In this opening chapter we took a look at the communications process and all that is going on between a sender and receiver. With all that is going on, it makes one marvel just how well we communicate most times without a lot of effort. But issues arise when the heat is turned up and differences arise. The rest of this book is to help you communicate well in such instances.

In Chapter 2, *Perception: The Map Is Not the Territory*, we explore perception as you most likely have never experienced before. Then in Chapter 3, *The Structure of Magic: Skillfully Communicating about* Differences, using your knowledge of perception as a solid foundation, we look at using effective communication patterns to help you: a) resolve the difference. That is, not necessarily to solve, but to come to a shared decision, and, b) perhaps move things to new and better places.

2. PERCEPTION: THE MAP IS NOT THE TERRITORY

The map is not the territory.

—Alfred Korzbyski

Everyone is "right" by his or her definition

—Alfred Korzbyski

You have a unique window of the world. Everyone does. It's through this window that you see and process the world. It determines how the world shows up for you.

And your view of the world is just that—your view of the world. Reality is out there. Reality is what is going on. And you are an interpreter of what is going on. You make your own unique translation based on your personal makeup and experiences.

Alfred Korzbyski captured this critical perception phenomenon so well with his phrase "the map is not the territory". The territory is out there in the real world. That is, "what he said", "what they did", "who she is", and so forth. And as you experience what is going on you become a mapmaker. The accuracy of your mapmaking may vary from reality a little bit or quite a lot, depending on a variety of factors.

PERCEPTION: THE MAP IS NOT THE TERRITORY

Alfred Korzbski[1], Sam Bois[2], S. I. Hayakawa[3], and William H. Pemberton[4], are the pioneers of what is called general semantics. *General semantics (or semantics) being a general theory and study of the human evaluative process.*[5]

Having established the importance of this perception principle, let's move on and get you involved. Exercise 2.1 below is the first exercise on a journey through this chapter on perception.

Exercise 2.1: What Do You See?

<u>What to Do</u>

1. Take a look at the three images[6] below and note what you see.
2. Turn to Appendix A, "Answers and Comments", **Exercise 2.1: What Do You See?**, page 75, to compare notes.

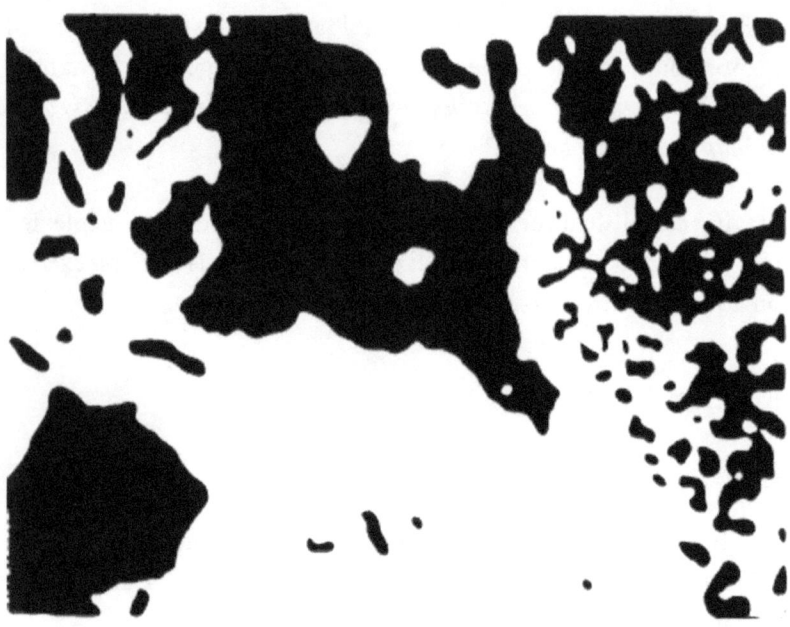

Exercise 2.1 involves an activity between your visual nerve endings and each of the three sketches. It is an example of the basic level of perception which involves making an observation of what is going on by using one or several of your senses: seeing, hearing, feeling tasting, or smelling. In this instance, seeing.

In working with Bill Pemberton in providing training sessions on communicating about differences, he would often get the attendees involved using their tasting sense.

Small strips of paper had been dipped ahead of time in a solution of phenyl-thio-carbamide. Each person was asked to wad their small strip up and swish it around in their mouth. People were then asked to talk about their experience. Some people tasted the paper as bitter; and some tasted nothing. Turns out that whether they are a taster or not comes with the gene. We will discuss the participants various responses to their experiences in a bit in conjunction with a valuable model that lays out the stages of personal mental development in the human evaluative process.

Now let's look at an example below[7]. This time involving the sense of feeling.

All of these experiments in perception involved only making maps of the territory using one of your senses. And I can attest that people can and have gotten quite worked up at this fundamental level as they argue about who was the right map.

When we move beyond the observation level and people begin to make broader maps using their unique backgrounds and beliefs you can appreciate that the differences in interpretations can become much more diverse. And when there is some ownership or emotion involved regarding the accuracy of mapmaking going on, you can further appreciate how the task of communicating about differences becomes a lot more difficult. That's why we are here.

Now let's go to the next exercise and ratchet things up a notch.

Exercise 2.2: Who Done It?[8]

<u>What to Do</u>

1. Read the brief story below. Assume that all the information in the story is accurate and true. You may refer back to the story if you wish.
2. Read each statement about the story. Determine whether each statement is:

   "T" – True
   "F" – False
   "?" – Not sure

   Circle your choice.

3. Turn to Appendix A, "Answers and Comments", **Exercise 2.2: Who Done It?**, page 76, to check your answers.

STORY

Babe Smith has been killed. Police have rounded up six suspects, all of whom are known gangsters. All of them are known to have been near the scene of the killing at the approximate time that it occurred. All had substantial motives for wanting Smith killed. However, one of these suspected gangsters, Slinky Sam, has positively been cleared of guilt.

STATEMENTS ABOUT STORY

1. Slinky Sam is known to have been near the scene of the killing of Babe Smith.   T   F   ?

2. All six of the rounded-up gangsters were known to have been near the scene of the crime.   T   F   ?

3. Only Slinky Sam has been cleared of guilt.   T   F   ?

4. All six of the rounded-up suspects were near the scene of Smith's killing at the approximate time it took place.   T   F   ?

5. The police do not know who killed Smith.   T   F   ?

6. All six suspects are known to have been near the scene of the foul deed.   T   F   ?

7. Smith's murderer did not confess of his own free will.   T   F   ?

8. Slinky Sam was not cleared of guilt.   T   F   ?

9. It is known that the six suspects were in the vicinity of the cold-blooded assassination.   T   F   ?

How did you do? Review your answers as you wish. But do not fret over it. This exercise is designed to have you distinguish between fact and inference.

THE LADDER OF INFERENCE

The exercise above provides a perfect transition for introducing an extremely valuable structure—The Ladder of Inference. The Ladder of Inference helps you develop an awareness of the various levels of inference or mapmaking you might engage in as you perceive what is going on.

FIGURE 2.1: The Ladder of Inference

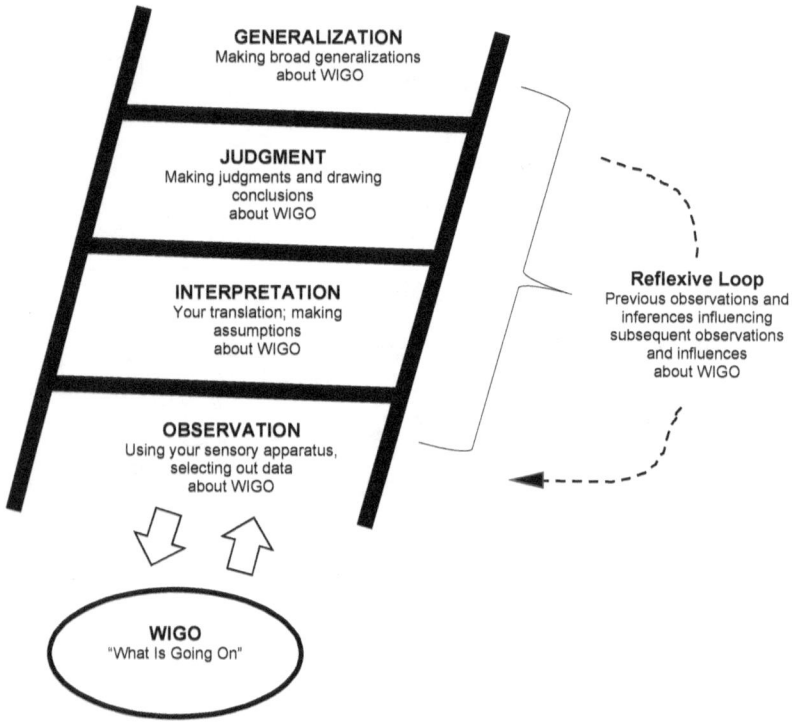

The Ladder of Inference demonstrates that as you ascend the various rungs of the ladder you make broader and broader maps of the territory, that is, WIGO. You go from sensing to postulating; from facts to assumptions. At the observation level your map may be very detailed. As you move beyond your sensory apparatus and factor more and more of you as a person into the evaluative process your map becomes sketchier. There is nothing wrong with this. It is natural. Even though your higher-level maps of inference will be increasingly more general, you still could be spot on with reality. Or, you may increasingly miss the mark as you ascend the rungs. But that is the beauty of this construct. It helps you be aware of your level of inferences. And, as appropriate, help you validate your assumptions.

Figure 2.2: Examples: The Ladder of Inference

	Example 1	Example 2	Example 3
Generalization	John is unreliable.	No wonder the rates are so high.	Mary can't keep up the pace, and so she's willing to have us lose our competitive edge.
Judgment	John always comes in late.	That is so nonproductive.	She can't compete very well.
Interpretation	John knew exactly when the meeting was to start. He deliberately came in late.	Must be a poor job of planning.	Mary doesn't like competition.
Observation	The meeting was called for 9 a.m. and John came at 9:30. He didn't say why he was late.	Look, there is a utility construction crew. One guy is working and the other three are standing around.	Mary says: "We need to find a way to reward people for the contribution they make to the whole".
WIGO			

In addition to serving as a useful construct to increase your understanding of the various levels of inference, The Ladder of Inference can be valuable to you in communicating key thoughts. Toward this end the ladder can be thought of as representing various levels of abstraction from specific to general. And it is important for you to *vary the level of abstraction* in your communications when you

COMMUNICATING ABOUT DIFFERENCES

are trying to make a point. That is, to go from the specific or data and facts, to the general, or conclusions and generalizations, and vice versa. To go from discussing DNP (Domestic National Product) to talking about meat and potatoes (marketplace elements that go into make up the DNP).

Figure 2.3: Varying Your Level of Abstraction

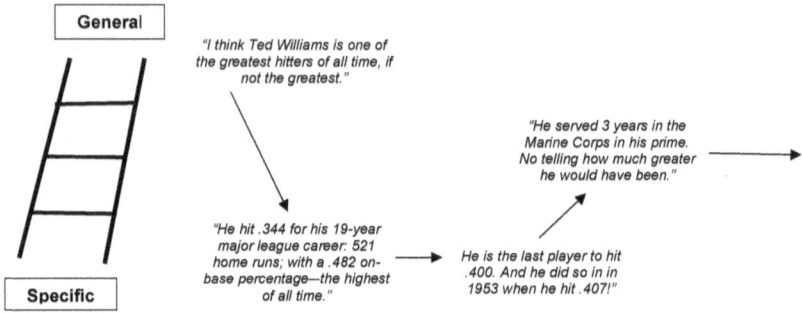

When you receive feedback like, "What's your point?", you are being asked to be more general, to summarize. When you hear "Give me an example", you are being asked to be more specific. In such instances, people are asking you to vary your level of abstraction to help them understand what you are trying to communicate. That's useful feedback.

Let us now turn our attention to furthering your understanding as to why you and everyone else have unique windows of the world and consequently make different maps of the same territory.

THE STRUCTURE OF INTERPRETATION

Figure 2.4: Structure of Interpretation

The Structure of Interpretation helps you understand and appreciate how the world shows up for you, and others.

In general semantics, a term referenced and defined earlier, Korzbyski, Bois, Hayakawa, and Pemberton, used the term Structural Differential to refer to this human evaluative model. I prefer the term Structure of Interpretation[9]. I believe it to be a more descriptive label. I have also redesigned the model and added a few embellishments, which I consider to be enhancements.

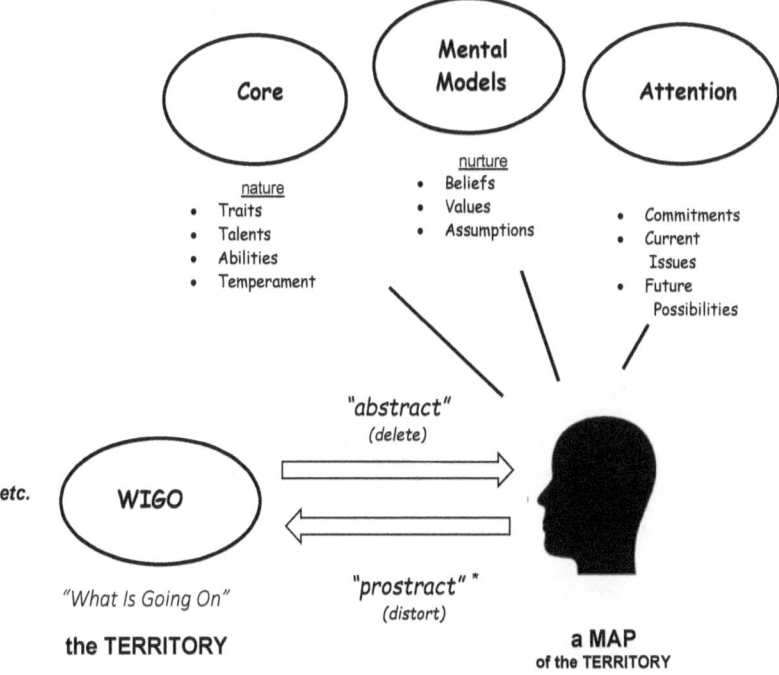

---

* Pemberton coined the word *prostract* to represent the fact that we project ourselves into our viewing of what is happening.

Understanding the Structure of Interpretation

The fact that reality and your perception of reality are two different things has been stressed thus far, and will continue to be. This perception principle is emphasized so heavily because it is so pivotal for you to be able to engage in genuine and effective conversation and dialogue regarding differences you encounter. Again, the "map is not the territory" metaphor is used to summarize this critical perception principle.

The Structure of Interpretation model allows us to dive into some detail to better understand this principle. How we view and process what is going on.

Let us now review the components of the model.

Abstracting and Prostracting

Through the Ladder of Inference, you saw how you can have varying levels of inference as you take in WIGO, "what is going on". (From here on the acronym WIGO will be used). These inferences start at the observation level and can progress to broader levels of assumptions and judgments as you ascend The Ladder of Inference.

The phenomenon of abstracting and prostracting adds to your understanding of what happens when you take in information in your mapmaking process.

When you *abstract* you form a map of what is going on. And in the process of making your map you *delete* some, or a lot, of what is really going on, depending on the complexity of the territory, your relevant knowledge, and the precision of your mapmaking.

In addition, as you make your map you also *prostract* or push yourself into what is going on in making your map. That is, with any life situation you project your accumulated experiences and beliefs from your own unique history. And in the process of doing so you can *distort* a little or a lot of what is actually going on.

Don't worry, there is nothing wrong about you deleting or distorting. It just happens, and is natural. Of course, with people who grossly delete or distort society needs to step in and do something.

Exercise 2.3: Deletion

What to Do

1. Count the number of Fs in the statement below.
2. Turn to Appendix A, "Answers and Comments", **Exercise, 2.3: Deletion**, page 77, to check your response.

> FINISHED FILES ARE THE RESULT OF
> YEARS OF SCIENTIFIC STUDY COMBINED
> WITH THE EXPERIENCE OF YEARS.

COMMUNICATING ABOUT DIFFERENCES

Exercise 2.4: Distortion

<u>What to Do</u>

1. Describe what you see in the picture below.
2. Turn to Appendix A, "Answers and Comments", **Exercise, 2.4: Distortion, page 77,** to check your response.

etc. is shown in the model to signify that there is always something more to be seen, heard, known or said about anything.

<u>Core</u>

Your core is what you came on the planet with. Your *natural* traits, talents, abilities, and temperament. Your unique DNA, sort of speak.

So, your core is hard wired, right? Well, yes and no. Your traits, talents, and abilities are. But the same does not apply to your temperament.

Your traits, that is, your inherited physical characteristics, are fixed. Your talents are your innate special physical or mental gifts. Your abilities, that is, your ultimate physical or mental capacity to do something, are also fixed. But something of importance needs to be pointed out here as it relates to talents and abilities. Think of your various talents and abilities as buckets. The *capacity* of some of these buckets is large. Others, not as large; or forgive me, perhaps rather small. Your natural physical and mental buckets do not increase with age. But, as you may have noticed, some of them decrease with age.

Think of your *competence* in any particular area as the current liquid level or your accumulated knowledge and skill in that area, that is any particular talent or ability bucket. Your capacity limits the ultimate level to which you can grow in that particular area. For example, you may love to play the piano, and have optimized your ability through dedication and deliberate practice. But no matter how much you try you may not have what it takes to make it to Carnegie Hall. But that's okay. You are just being realistic. And such a realization does not interfere with the enjoyment you get in tinkling the ivories and fine tuning your musical ability.

Your current competence in any particular area will ebb and flow depending on how much you attend to your knowledge and skill level in that area. The level will increase as you gain additional knowledge and hone your skills. By the same token your acumen and skill level may decrease if you do not keep up and get rusty.

This distinction between talent and ability, that is, capacity and current competence, is a valuable distinction. Perhaps it is a real insight for you. A related thought. *Wisdom* can be defined as practical know-how based on experience.

Now turning to temperament. Like your traits, talents and abilities are natural. They are innate. But unlike your traits, talents, and abilities your temperament is not necessarily fixed. Your temperament can be somewhat malleable. If so motivated, through attention, deliberate practice, and application you can modify your natural priorities and preferences to adapt to different situations and people you encounter.

For example, think back to the DISC behavioral style model we discussed in Chapter 1. Let's say that you are a project manager and *your natural behavioral style is Steadiness (S)*. You prefer the collaborative approach.

But you realize the benefits of *adapting* to the various other behavioral styles of the people you constantly interact with in your role as project manager. Such adapting increases your communication effectiveness and develops constructive relationships as you work through important project opportunities and challenges.

When interacting on important matters with a person who's natural, most likely subconscious, preference is a *Dominant (D) behavioral style* you might do such things as get to the point; agree on goals and boundaries; discuss results, winning strategies, and action steps; provide concise data; avoid details and focus on the big picture.

With an Influential (I) behavioral style you might emphasize the people aspects of your project; be optimistic and upbeat; demonstrate, if deserved, that you admire in them; be in touch with and support their feelings; interact and participate with them; avoid details; and, keep a fast, lively approach.

With a Conscientiousness (C) behavioral style you might approach them in a nonthreatening way; demonstrate your reasoning; provide assurances; provide explanations, data, and proof; allow them to exercise due diligence before proceeding; compliment them on their thoroughness and correctness; and, allow them to find the best solution or correct answer within limits.

When interacting with another Steadiness (S) behavioral style you obviously will not have to do much in the way of adapting in that you share the same style. Sometimes however it is useful to take on another style so the two of you can test out other ways of thinking and add to the quality of your thinking.

You must realize that any thinking or behavioral model, no matter how well researched and useful, does not begin to predict or explain the uniqueness and complexity of you or anyone. But the use of the DISC model, which is an excellent model of behavioral styles, allows you to make the distinction between natural and adaptive approaches to increase your interpersonal effectiveness.

Mental Models

Whereas your core is natural to you, your mental models are learned and developed as you experience life. They are nurtured. The beliefs, values, and assumptions that comprise your mental models come from the multiplicity of experiences and influences you have had and will continue to have as you lived life. Some have made deep and lasting impressions on you. Others not so much. Still others have faded, but perhaps are still there in your subconscious.

These life experiences and influences include such things as your early years; how you were raised; marriage; parenting; schooling; athletics; clubs and associations; religion; communities you have lived in; the military; work experiences; and teachers, mentors, coaches and other people who may have cared about and helped you.

Peter Senge defines mental models as:

> *Deeply ingrained assumptions, generalizations, or even pictures or images that influence how we understand the world and how we take action.*[10]

COMMUNICATING ABOUT DIFFERENCES

Some of these mental models can get every bit as hard wired as your core. And when people of like persuasion bond together there is the potential for major impact, good or bad.

In her book *Caste* Isabel Wilkerson writes about caste systems in general, and specifically the caste systems of India, Nazi Germany, and the United States. She states that:

> *Caste is more than rank, it is a state of mind that holds everyone captive, the dominant imprisoned in an illusion of their own entitlement, the subordinate trapped in the purgatory of someone else's definition of who they are and who they should be.*[11]

For our purposes we can substitute the term social stratification to refer to this phenomenon of classifying and rating groups or people based on such things as their ethnicity, race, religion, wealth, sex, sexual preference, political affiliation or some other mental model that automatically and arbitrarily decides that some groups or people inferior to others.

When people with intense shared persuasions bond together a tribal mentality often occurs, leading to cult-like behavior.

We know all know too well the pernicious effects that can result when groups with "us versus them" rigid states of mind operate exclusively from within their own bubble and see outsiders as the enemy. Rather than working together with diverse groups and people and collaborating regarding various points of view to find common ground for the greater good, such insular and myopic thinking leads to attacking and sometimes brutalizing or persecuting non-believers or people who are different.

In his book *Why We're Polarized* Ezra Klein speaks to the political polarization that has overtaken the United States. He cites extreme political identity and to a somewhat lesser degree issue identity as the primary causes of this malaise. These insular and myopic identities have been growing in the recent past, and the divide has deepened as the left moves more to the left and the right moves more to the right. The result is a dysfunctional congress, a delegitimizing of some of our democratic institutions, and a fierce loyalty to party rather than working together to do the right thing for the country. Compromise has become a dirty word.[12]

Sorry to take our mental model discussion to such an ugly place. But you need to understand just how powerful mental models can be in driving individual and group thinking and behavior.

But let's get back to you as an individual. You and I are probably not going to change the world. Nor do we necessarily want to. But rather than curse the darkness, we can light individual candles in our own unique spheres of influence. We can model the way by being authentic and seeking to understand others. That does not mean that we have to agree with them. But it does mean that we are open to differences and try to understand them.

To continually improve as a positive influence, you need to continually strive for a higher level of consciousness by getting to know yourself better. You want to continually examine your mental models and, as appropriate, revise them based on new realities and what you have learned.

And when wanting to make positive change you need to realize that you are a product of the mental models you carry around and the practices you engage in. This is an extremely valuable point for you to understand. So, in making positive change you not only need to revise some of your mental models (your thinking), but also engage in practices (your behavior) that will allow you to act in ways that will represent the new you. We will talk more about self-coaching in Appendix B, "Putting It to Work: Crafting Improvement Strategies".

In getting to a higher level of consciousness and gaining greater clarity of your purpose, a good question to ask yourself and do some serious reflection on is: "Who would I be if nobody ever told me who I should be?"

Attention

What is on your mind, be they "in the moment" issues or concerns, or short-term or long-term concerns, hopes or ambitions, also affect your perception of WIGO. And it cuts both ways.

If you are currently keenly interested in something and that subject is being discussed you perk up and tune in. Conversely, your preoccupation with something that is on your mind can substantially interfere with your understanding of WIGO as you tune out, temporarily or longer.

Exercise 2.5: Your Structure of Interpretation

Purpose

Provide an opportunity to achieve a higher order of consciousness for yourself. Gain greater clarity regarding how the world shows up for you and why it does so.

What to Do

1. On a sheet of paper form three columns and label the columns: Core, Mental Models, and Attention.

2. In each column write down the key characteristics that define you. What are the key determinants that affect how you make your maps of the territory? You may not have much to say in the Attention column. But you should have a lot to say in the Core and Mental Model columns.
3. Review your work and do some serious reflection. What key insights have you gained? Did this exercise trigger any modifications you may want to make?

Use the Structure of Interpretation on an ongoing basis to increase your self-awareness. Also use it to help you better understand others.

Social Intelligence

An understanding and use of the Structure of Interpretation can greatly increase what I call your social intelligence.

I define *social intelligence* as an awareness of self and others, and using such awareness to enhance effective communications and build meaningful relationships.

Instead of social intelligence, Daniel Goleman uses the term emotional intelligence in his pioneering and valuable work to refer to this important concept[13]. I prefer the term social intelligence. It is not as limiting to me in understanding and explaining this important concept. Goleman argues that emotional intelligence can matter more than raw intelligence in determining one's human effectiveness. In other words, EQ (Emotional Quotient) is more important than IQ (Intelligence Quotient).

STAGES OF AWARENESS

In viewing the world and processing experiences in general, or specific topics or issues, you run into a variety of folks with different levels of tolerance with viewpoints that differ from yours. On one end of the spectrum, you run into people who are locked into their maps. On the other end of the spectrum, there are those who are tolerant and respectful of divergent points of view. They are willing to revise their maps based on new realities, new learning, or reaching a higher level of consciousness. We are not talking about "wishy-washy" people here. Or what politicians call "flip flopping" when they want to demean other politicians because they altered their views on an issue.

Carol Dweck in her book *mindsets* uses the term *fixed mindset* to refer to those who are not open to divergent points of view and learning. She uses the term *growth mindset* to refer those who are open to new and diverse inputs, divergent points of view, continuous learning and perhaps changing their way of thinking based upon such inputs and experiences.[14]

Pemberton with a model he calls the Sanity Spectrum allows us to deepen our understanding regarding the various developmental stages that exist in the human evaluative process.[15]

I prefer to call this invaluable human developmental model, shown below, Stages of Awareness. I have also taken the liberty of making a few additions to add to the comprehensiveness and understanding of the model. I know Bill would approve.

Figure 2.5: Stages of Awareness

Stage	Personal Mental Development	Philosophical Viewpoint or Orientation	Personal Identification	Handling Conflict
I	Infant Sensing Dependence	There are no other viewpoints.	"me"	Withdraw
II	Child *"You're OK... I'm not OK"* Classifying Dependence	**ABSOLUTISTIC** Two-valued orientation, i.e., either/or; right/wrong; good/bad, etc. The quality is in the thing.	"like me"	"One way"
III	Youth/ Parent *I'm OK... you're not OK"* Relating Independence	**RELATIVISTIC** I determine what is real, best, right, good, etc. I determine the quality.	"like us"	"Many ways—but, one right way"
IV	Adult *"I'm OK... you're OK"*[16] Postulating Interdependence	**TRANSITORY** Multi-valued orientation. The map is not the territory. It is just a map.	"like anyone"	"Many ways—so let's compare notes and come up with the best way."

There is a lot in this model. Real good stuff.

Let's enliven the model and deepen your understanding of it by using a real-life example.

We will draw upon the example used earlier in this chapter. To review, Pemberton used chemically treated paper wads and had group participants chew on a wad and discuss their experiences. To some the paper tasted bitter. To others it was tasteless. Whether a person was a taster or not came with the gene.

The exercise was used to emphasize the map is not the territory perception principle. We will now use the typical sorts of responses the participants had to illustrate the differences between Stages II, III, and IV in the evaluative process as shown in the Stages of Awareness model. A Stage I type typical response is not included because such people are not likely to be, and were not, part of such an exercise. They could not relate to what is going on.

Figure 2.6: Bitter or Not Bitter?

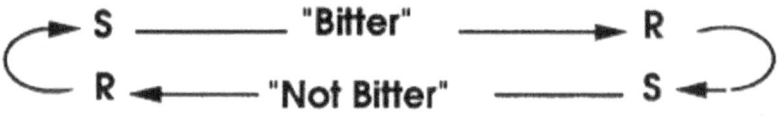

S = Sender or Situation
R = Receiver or Response

Stage I	*Not applicable.* See comment related to Stage I responses above.
Stage II *Absolutistic*	The quality is in the thing. Therefore, taste is in the chemical. Interpretation: The other person has a different piece of paper; or has faulty taste buds. Standard talk: "Go back and taste it again."
Stage III *Relativistic*	The taste is determined by me. Interpretation: We may be different. Standard talk: "No big deal. I'm telling it the way it is."
Stage IV *Transitory*	There is a transaction going on between the chemical on the paper and my taste buds. Interpretation: Curious about why we have different reactions, and why. Standard talk: "I did/didn't taste it." "What about you?" "We had different reactions." "I wonder what is going on?"

With your understanding of the Stages of Awareness model, you realize that the lower the development stage of the person you have a difference with, the tougher the communication challenge is for you. A person with a firm or fixed mind set, either in general or with regard to the issue or topic under discussion, is not interested or capable of engaging in a genuine conversation on the subject. They typically go into a flight or fight mode. And if they do enter the discussion it usually will be in the form of a debate, not a conversation.

This is a good place to identify and define the different kinds of interactions that can occur.

Figure 2.7: Categories of Interaction

	Debate	Polite Discussion	Skillful Conversation	Dialogue
Intent	To change another's views or assumptions. To win.	To come to some sort of closure.	To resolve; make a decision; reach agreement; identify priorities.	Create a setting where shared understanding can be achieved. Understand one another. Explain; discover; develop insight.
Meaning	"to beat down"		"to shake apart"	"to turn together"

Monologue: One-way communications. Duologue: Simultaneous monologues.

The ground rules for effective dialogue include:

- Treat each other as colleagues.
- People will not have remarks attributed to them outside our conversation unless we agree to it.
- Right and wrong are not a concern.
- Injection of new perspectives is encouraged.
- No sarcasm.
- Treat everyone with respect.

Korzybski maintained that we slip away from sanity to the degree we fail to make distinctions between different levels of abstracting as we make our maps. He laid this out on a hypothetical distribution as shown below with the vast majority of people at Stages II and III.[17]

Figure 2.8: Sanity Model

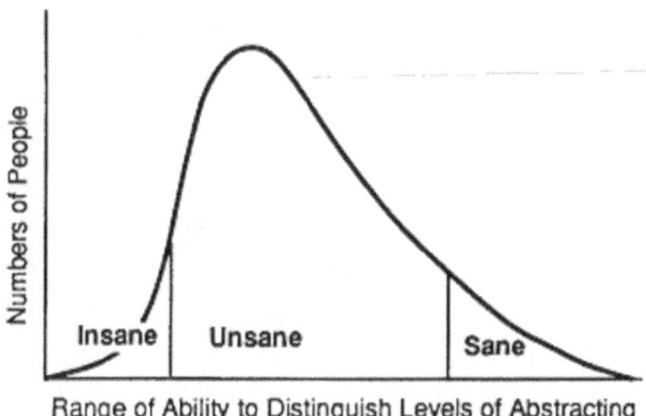

| Stages Of Awareness: | I | II | III | IV |

Using Korsybski's Sanity Model as a focus, let's explore some of the implications.

- A young child typically cannot interact beyond Stage I when differences occur. *"It's mine"! "No, it's mine"!*

- As the child ages, hopefully she will grow mentally as well as physically. To go from Stage II to Stage III, and possibly to Stage IV. This of course takes time. To move beyond a fixed mindset toward a growth mindset involves getting to know oneself and developing the requisite social intelligence, along with skillful talk patterns.

- Some people may not have the ability to grow beyond Stage II.

- Other people, for whatever reason, may opt to stay at Stage II, electing not to continuously learn and grow. Most times this occurs at a subconscious level.

They may feel comfortable in what they perceive to be a sheltered environment and not have their assumptions challenged or have to revise them in light of new and emerging realities. They will tend to surround themselves with people "like me" or "like us" and otherwise become withdrawn.

- As we live our lives we all form allegiances with people and groups. Hopefully these associations give us satisfaction and perhaps help us learn and grow. But for some people these associations stiffle who they are. They are not open and honest in the midst of such affiliations. They are fearful that if they are authentic and be open and honest, they will suffer the consequences. They will be embarrassed, ridiculed, lose status, suffer career consequences, or be ostracized.

- And going a step, or several steps, further, some people become so consumed with individuals and groups that such affiliations become a large part of their identity. Anyone or anything that rubs up against such affiliations the wrong way is seen as the enemy. Forget about social intelligence. So sad.

So, what is to be done to help individuals engulfed in the last situation described? When who they are is largely defined by such unhealthy associations and they become blinded to any countervailing opinions. They shut down.

Most of these folks are otherwise intelligent and you would think they could see what they got themselves into. And the fact of the matter is that most of them do. Think about the people you see, hear or read about in public view who you know are lying, and they do to. What will it take for them to get real?

For some of them education and enlightenment may work. But for most, until the driving forces to change outweigh the restraining forces to hang on to such beliefs, regardless if they believe them or not, they will not change. They fear too much for their own hides rather than risk to do the right thing for the greater good.

So, what should your role be in trying to help these people see the light? Probably nothing, unless you think that shedding a little enlightenment might be helpful. But don't overdo it. People do not want to be told how to think and what to do. If they do see themselves clearly and have the necessary fortitude and courage, they can move themselves forward. But, as previously mentioned, you can do good in your own sphere of influence and have a positive effect by modeling the way through your social intelligence.

The same thing needs to be said about nudging the hypothetical distribution curve in the sanity model to the right. None of us are going to be able to have a large impact on the whole. But locally there is hope. And as you model the way at the local level, that is your family, friends, and community, you may have an impact far greater than you think. But don't wait for people to come up and say "Thanks for helping me raise my level of consciousness". That's just not the way it works most times.

Where We Are

We started things off in Chapter 1 my going into some depth regarding the communications process and some of the implications for you.

We then moved to this chapter and did a rather thorough job of exploring perception and social intelligence, which are vital if you are going to have genuine conversations and dialogues when important differences occur. The "map is not the territory" is such a valuable metaphor to constantly remind you that your perception of what is going on and what is really going on are two different things.

Four powerful models—the Ladder of Abstraction; the Structure of Interpretation; Stages of Awareness; and Sanity Model—were reviewed. Your understanding of these models definitely help in continually moving to higher levels of social intelligence.

In the next chapter we discuss and practice effective communication patterns to be used in communicating about differences. These communication patterns allow you to capably demonstrate the higher levels of social awareness in seeking to understand and be understood. Hopefully, these effective communication patterns will become more and more a part of you and help you grow into an even better you.

3. THE STRUCTURE OF MAGIC: SKILLFULLY COMMUNICATING ABOUT DIFFERENCES

There is not too much you can't say if you say it right.

The Principle of Reciprocity (or Caring)*:*
If you think I am trying to understand you, you may be indebted to try and understand me.

—William Pemberton

Getting Grounded

A good place to start before we explore the skillful communication patterns that are so critical to meaningful conversations about differences is to provide you with three recommendations to help you get focused for any difficult conversations that come your way.

You need to be mindful of this first recommendation whenever you communicate about differences. It is based on an outline developed by Pemberton.

Figure 3.1: The 3 Rs of Effective Communication

Role	• "What is my role in this situation?" • "Should I leave well enough alone; or, would directly addressing the issue be appropriate for me to do?" • "What are my authorities in this situation?" "Can I can make anything happen." "I can influence." If I can't influence, drop it. • "Speak up now or at some other opportune time?" • "Who are the key stakeholders?" • "What are the consequences of doing nothing?"
Risk	*Effective communication is risky. You never know what you are going to find or where things might go when you seek to understand and be authentic about yourself when discussing differences.* *To effectively deal with resistance and differences, you have to be willing to take a risk, and the time and effort to actively listen and assertively communicate.*
Responsibility	*Being willing and able to clean up any messes you might create by reaching out to effectively deal with issues and being authentic. You want to approach the interaction with a "win-win" or "both/and" versus a "win-lose" or zero-sum attitude. What you are trying to do is get the real issues out on the table and to see what is possible. In doing so, you will use your communication skills to try and keep both you and the others you are interacting with whole.*

The second recommendation is a technique to be used "in the moment". You take a quick time out and get yourself centered. You get yourself to neutral by closing your eyes, literally or figuratively, and taking a few deep breaths. You do this before such instances as making an important phone call or speaking up about your concerns at a meeting. Really, whenever you are about to enter into a potentially difficult situation.

Once you begin to incorporate this practice into your normal routine you will be surprised how quickly you can get centered, including in the middle of a meeting. The term "freeze frame"[1] is a good descriptor of what you want to accomplish in calling your brief time out. Because what you are doing is stopping the action right on the set, sort of speak to, get collected.

A third recommendation is to whenever you have time to prepare for a difficult conversation, to outline your communication plan by thinking through the following:

- What's my objective?
- What's my strategy?
    - Basic approach.
    - Key messages.
    - When and where to have the communication.
    - Who should be present?
    - What is/are the natural behavioral styles of the person/people I will be meeting with? What is the best way to adapt to such styles?

- Communication patterns.
    - Think about what you want to say and how to say it.
    - Think about possible reactions and how to prepare for such reactions.
    - Don't get too scripted however. You don't want to come off as being too canned. And, once you get started with the meeting it may go places you haven't anticipated. You need to be flexible.

TALK CHAIN

The talk chain is a very valuable construct and serves well in introducing communication patterns. Communication patterns that can get in the way of attempting to talk about differences; and communication patterns that can be effective.

Figure 3.2: Talk Chain

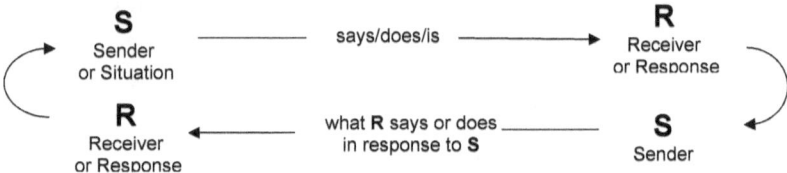

If R is okay with what or who S says, does, or is, or WIGO, everything is cool. But if R is insulted or otherwise knocked off balance by what S says, does, or is, or WIGO, then how R responses is pivotal as to whether or not the talk chain stays open and any constructive communication can occur.

But before introducing the ineffective and effective communication patterns in tough situations, let's take a quick, but very much related, detour.

Principles or laws from various people are scattered throughout this book. "The map is not the territory" being an example. These sage sayings say a lot in a few words and serve to highlight and summarize the topic being discussed.

Below are some laws that fit here.

> Law of Insult: *I am a partial author of any insult I give or receive.*
>
> —William H. Pemberton

> (I don't know. Maybe my standards are too finicky. Or maybe it's the way I came across.)

> Law of Choice: *It may be wrong for me to assume that a person could have behaved any differently in a given situation.*
>
> —William H. Pemberton

> (Who knows. If I was in his shoes, I may have done the same thing.)

> Law of Assumed Benevolence: *It is probably safe to assume that the vast majority of people do not want to intentionally insult or hurt me.*
>
> —Dan Fischer

> (They have enough problems of their own.)

Figure 3.3 below lists natural response and skilled responses in communicating about differences.

Figure 3.3: Natural and Skilled Responses

Natural Responses Can Hinder

Responses that tend to get in the way of constructively talking about differences

- Sullen silence
- Attack
- Deceiving

Skilled Responses Can Help

Responses that can facilitate meaningful conversation about differences

Active Listening
- Attending and Acknowledging
- Inquiry
- Paraphrase/Speculate

Assertive Communication
- Describing
- Stating Thoughts
- Stating Feelings

Natural Responses: The SAD Syndrome

Pemberton identified these typical natural responses of people in crisis and labeled these responses the Sad Syndrome. "SAD" is formed by taking the first letter of each of the three typical responses. And if that all a person can do in uncomfortable situations, that is, clam-up, whack back, or make a joke, it is indeed sad.

Figure 3.4: Natural Responses in Crisis

Sullen silence
"anger-inners"
"clamming up". "copping-out"
pouting child
passive-aggressive
Contrasted with the silence of listening

Attack	"anger-outers" whacking back judgments; advice; blaming "YOU" messages
Deceiving	fraud; phony; making light incongruities between feeling and talk passive-aggressive

The big problem with these natural responses in crisis is that they tend to invalidate or cancel out the other person in the situation. And in so doing, such natural responses are likely to trigger natural responses on the part of the other person. The net effect is that the talk chain shuts down.

Principle of Imbalance (or Hyperexis):	*The very thing I do when insulted or knocked off balance emotionally or psychologically to get myself back in balance often times makes things worse.*
	—William H. Pemberton

Hyperexis is a Greek word meaning "fever". It is commonly used in the field of psychology. But the vast majority of us would rather be in a state of balance or homeostasis, that is, "static man".

Skilled Responses: The Structure of Magic[2]

Whereas natural responses tend to interfere with or shut down the chances of having any meaningful conversation in attempting to communicate about differences, skilled responses have the opposite effect. Skilled responses tend to keep the talk chain open. They tend not to invalidate the other person.

Skilled responses provide a structure of magic consisting of active listening and assertive communications, each with their various subsets. And when you want to start the conversation out on the right foot, or make a corrective adjustment when your natural responses are getting in the way, they act as a Rosetta Stone* or touch stone.

ACTIVE LISTENING: SKILLED RESPONSES

Attending and Acknowledging

To establish any kind of rapport with the speaker you need to demonstrate that you are present and care. You do so by attending to and acknowledging the speaker. You could actually be very much attuned to what the speaker is trying to communicate, but if you do not demonstrate your attentiveness or appear to be preoccupied or apathetic you are not going to engage the speaker.

You demonstrate your presence by making eye contact and utterances such as *"I see"*; *"really?"*; *"oh?"*; *"uh-huh"*; *"okay"*; *"wow"*; *and*, *"yea"*. There may be some inflection in your voice, but for the most part probably a fairly steady tone.

Inquiry

Inquiry is asking questions and gathering information. When inquiring you are consulting the speaker to better understand or clarify, as necessary and appropriate, the speaker's message.

---

* An inscribed stone found near Rosetta (now called Rashid) on the western mouth of the Nile in Egypt in 1799. Its text is written in three scripts: hieroglyphic, demotic, and Greek. The deciphering of the hieroglyphics by Jean-Francois Champolion in 1822 led to the interpretation of many other early records of many other early Egyptian civilizations. (Oxford Dictionary of English)

THE STRUCTURE OF MAGIC: SKILLFULLY COMMUNICATING ABOUT DIFFERENCES

> *The most important thing in communication is to hear what isn't being said.*
>
> —Peter F. Drucker

Your voice or tone is important in asking questions. You want a tone that comes across as being non-judgmental and inquisitive. You are asking for a reason—to better understand the speaker.

But aren't you interrupting when inquiring? Good question. The key is that as long as you keep the agenda with the speaker your probe most times will be interrupted as constructive and not interrupting in that you are seeking to understand and not to divert or take over the conversation. When you start putting in your own two cents, such as "Let me tell you about a similar situation I had", and the like, your line of inquiry most likely be perceived as interrupting. This is an important distinction. So, keep the agenda with the speaker.

There are two types of inquiry: closed-ended questions and open-ended questions. You probably have heard of these two types of probes.

Closed inquiries are designed to elicit short definitive responses, often with just a "yes" or "no" rely.

Examples: *"Do you think you're making progress?"*
"How long have you been working for him?"

Closed inquiries can be valuable in that you can gather appropriate information in a short time.

Open inquiries are designed to have the speaker express herself on regarding a question you have.

Examples: *"Can you describe for me what that looks like."*
"Could you give me an example of such an instance?"
"How does that occur?"

When inquiring, *avoid the "why?" question*. Why is that? Well even though the word "why" is certainly an inquiry, it often is inferred by the receiver that you are judging. That you thinking that he could have or should have done something different. *"Why did you do that?"*

Paraphrasing/Speculating

Paraphrasing/speculating is translating in your own words what you think the speaker's meaning, feeling, or motive, or all three, is. You are checking out your understanding of the message.

For example:
"You're puzzled about what to do next".
"You just want to talk this out."
"You're surprised and shocked about what happened."

Paraphrasing is not repeating back words verbatim like a recorder. Mirroring is not paraphrasing/speculating. What you are trying to do is verify your understanding of the essence of the message briefly in your own words.

Avoid starter phrases such as: *"In other words…"; "I hear you saying that…"; "If I'm reading you right…", and so forth.* Such phrases are not needed. The sender knows what you are trying to do, that is, capture their meaning, feeling, or motive. Not only are starter phrases not necessary, but they are a turn off when repeated. Get right to your translation.

By all means avoid being judgmental in voicing your translation.

When speculating you are going beyond paraphrasing. You are taking your translation and interpreting what you think the <u>real</u> meaning, feeling or motive is even though it was not distinctly expressed.

Figure 3.5: Distinguishing between Paraphrasing and Speculating

Paraphrasing	**Surface Level**	Translating in your own words what you think the speaker's meaning, feeling, or motive is.
	⬇	
Speculating	**Deep Level**	Intuiting about the speaker's *real* meaning, feeling, or motive even though not distinctly expressed.

The following is an example of the difference between a surface level and deep level translation.

A caring mother tells her teenage daughter:

"*I don't like the way your hair looks.*" (Surface Level)

Maybe her concern is something more than the hair. Perhaps the real concern is:

"*I really love you, and I don't want you to look foolish.*" (Deep Level)

Depending on the complexity and length of the message, you may need to go around the talk chain several times before the sender thinks or feels that you have captured the essence of what he was trying to communicate. Each round represents a successive approximation.

A good analogy can be drawn from my days in the military as part of a mortar squad. The squad consisted of a lead, a forward observer, a gunner, and a loader. The forward observer would use his special binoculars to focus on the target. The binoculars had a horizontal and vertical scale in yards. The forward observer would look through the binoculars at the target. A test round would be fired. Based on where the test round landed in relation to the target, the forward observer would provide feedback to the lead such as *"drop 75 (yards); right 50 (yards)"*. The lead would pass the direction on to the gunner who would make the adjustments. It may take several single round firings until the mortar tube was dialed in to the target. When that was the case, the forward observer would feed back *"Fire for effect"*. Multiple mortars would be fired in rapid succession until the target was wiped out.

And that is what happens when you take several trips around the talk chain in an attempt to zero in on the sender's message. But instead of saying "fire for effect", she says something like: *"That's right"*.

When trying to understand an involved or complex message, you will never get 100% of the meaning, feeling, or motive. If you did you would be that person. The person you are attempting to communicate with will determine when you are close enough.

In using active listening skilled responses, you are involved as an interested listener, an adult friend, or someone with a different, or potentially different, point of view.

As an interested listener you are attracted to the topic or the speaker, or both. As an adult friend you respect the speaker, so you naturally perk up a bit when he is speaking. As someone with a different point of view you want to listen so that you may learn something or present your thinking.

In your adult friend role, you can be of great service just by being present for the sender. Sometimes that is all he wants. He just wants to vent. In such cases, you limit yourself to attending and acknowledging. Most times however he wants you to try to understand him and demonstrate that you are trying to do so. In so doing, you may allow him to gain greater perspective, clarity, or insight relative to his issue or concern. And sometimes he may welcome some coaching about what to do. More on that in a moment.

In voicing a divergent point of view, in addition to using active listening skilled responses, when you speak up you will use assertive communication skilled responses to attempt to have a meaningful discussion or perhaps a dialogue about your real or perceived differences. We will discuss the assertive communication natural responses once we have ended our current discussion regarding the active listening skilled responses.

Working through an example

Let us work through an example illustrating skilled active listening responses and working around the talk chain.

The situation: You have a colleague who wants to discuss on important issue with you that is bothering him. He has told you that you are not personally involved, but that he would appreciate talking about the issue with you.

COMMUNICATING ABOUT DIFFERENCES

Your colleague	You
	When you meet you say that you would be happy to help. You ask what role your colleague would want you to play.
Says he would like you to hear him out.	
	You agree. But you wonder if your colleague just wants to vent or wants you to seek to understand what's going on with him regarding the issue. So, you ask.
He says that trying to understand just what is going on would be appreciated and perhaps be quite helpful.	
	You agree.
	You remind yourself that in seeking to understand you will avoid natural responses. Doing such things as: judging: *"Do you think you are overreacting?"*. Or, advising: *"I wouldn't worry about it."*. Or, interrupting by taking the agenda away from your colleague: *"I had a similar situation once, and what I did is…"*.
	What you need to do is use the skilled responses to seek to understand your colleague's real meaning, feeling or issue. Of course, you will be attentive. You will inquire when needed to gather relevant information to help your understanding. And you will paraphrase/speculate to check out your understanding and demonstrate your interest in doing so.
He describes the problem that has been gnawing at him for some time. It involves a procedure at work that he thinks needs to be modified. He also describes that people who initially backed the change have not come through. He goes into some detail.	

Your colleague	You
	You say:
	"You're stymied". (paraphrase)
	"And you're frustrated and perhaps feel a little betrayed that the support you thought you had has not materialized". (speculate)
He says that is pretty accurate. He says that he hasn't given up hope, and thinks there are some people who he could still possibly rely on to make it happen.	
	Having demonstrated your understanding you realize that you have probably already been quite helpful to your colleague, although he may not express it.
	At this point you think about whether or not your colleague would be receptive to you expanding your role. Specifically, to go beyond demonstrating understanding and moving into coaching.
	So, you inquire: *"Do you want to discuss possible next steps?"*

We will end the example here. Hopefully it was useful.

But this is an opportune time to discuss coaching.

Whether the sender has already expressed interest in receiving some help on how best to proceed or, as in the example above, it arises as a realistic inquiry, the place to start any coaching is to seek to understand just what is going on.

Coaching

Coaching is helping people help themselves regarding something they want to work on. It could be to solve a problem, make a decision, or craft a course of action to improve a situation or to personally develop in a specific area.

Coaching is about *"asking"*, not *"telling"*. There are times when being directive is the proper approach, but providing coaching is not one of them.

The Coaching Spectrum shown below is a useful scale to help you gauge your use of questions when coaching, and the degree to which you may be influencing the direction of your coaching.

Figure 3.6: The Coaching Spectrum

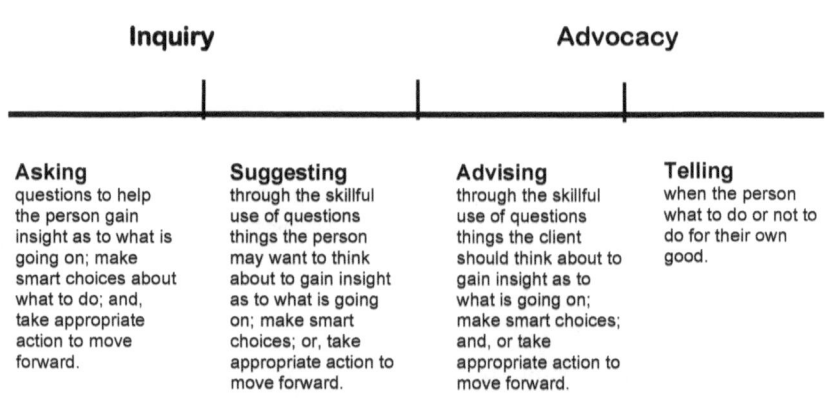

Inquiry			Advocacy
Asking questions to help the person gain insight as to what is going on; make smart choices about what to do; and, take appropriate action to move forward.	**Suggesting** through the skillful use of questions things the person may want to think about to gain insight as to what is going on; make smart choices; or, take appropriate action to move forward.	**Advising** through the skillful use of questions things the client should think about to gain insight as to what is going on; make smart choices; and, or take appropriate action to move forward.	**Telling** when the person what to do or not to do for their own good.

In providing coaching you want to try and stick with the Inquiry end of the spectrum, regardless of how tempting it may be to thrust yourself into the situation by advocating certain things. You can help the person you are coaching much more if you help her think things through for herself. In so doing there is greater chance she will own the decision, making it far more likely that she will do something with it.

After you get a chance to practice the active listening skills in the exercises below, we will move on to discussing and practicing the assertive communication skills.

ACTIVE LISTENING SKILLS: PRACTICE

These practice exercises are to help you better understand and use the skillful active listening responses.

Exercise 3.1: Identifying the Most Useful Response

<u>What to do</u>

Assume that each statement below was made to you early in a conversation in which the speaker was expressing a concern. Do the following:

1. Select the response you think would be the most useful in communicating with the speaker.
2. Compare your answers to those shown in Appendix A, "Answers and Comments", **Exercise, 3.1: Identifying the Most Useful Response**, pages 78, 79.

<u>Statements</u>

1. "I can't stand that new boss of mine. He's such an arrogant know-it-all. Everything that goes wrong he puts on me."

    a. "I guess all of us have a tough time breaking in a new boss."
    b. "Tell me what sort of things have been happening."

2. "I'm really fed up with these reports. It looks like everything has to be done yesterday. Why can't we get a little more notice? There's no way to do a good job. What's so tough is

that we spend a lot of time getting information that nobody is really going to use."

    a. "You find it hard to keep interested in doing a good job when you feel like you're under pressure to produce stuff that nobody uses."
    b. "You shouldn't feel that way. It's your job. And if something's not right, fix it."

3. "I'm running into some real problems with my group since I got promoted. It's hard to figure out how to relate to the people I used to work with, but now work for me."

    a. "How long have you had the new job?"
    b. "So, the relationship with the people you worked with has become strained since you became their boss."

Exercise 3.2: Describe Appropriate Response

<u>What to Do</u>

1. Specifically state what you would say when faced with each of the statements below that would stand a good chance of keeping the talk chain open.
2. Compare your responses to those shown in Appendix A, "Questions and Answers", **Exercise, 3.2: Identify Appropriate Response**, pages 80, 81.

<u>Statements</u>

1. "I'm sorry I am late for our meeting again. I really tried to be on time, but I have a lot going on at home."

2. You thought you had made your wishes clear. But then you are told the following:

"I didn't know you wanted this done today. You never made that clear I thought we were going to talk about it in detail first."

3. You are about to start a meeting with a small group you have never met before, and you are hit with the following:

"The last time we had one of these things nothing happened afterwards. All the things we agreed on were forgotten. These things are a waste of time."

4. You come home from a hard day at work, and your spouse greets you with:

"What a day I've had. The baby was crying all morning. The washing machine broke down, and I had to do things by hand. Then I went downtown to buy a hat and I had to wait 20 minutes for a bus. I couldn't find a thing I liked and everybody was so pushy and the store was so crowded. When I got back the baby sitter had the stew burnt—and I had worked so hard on it. I'm so mad I could cry. And I've got to go downtown again tomorrow."

ASSERTIVE COMMUNICATION

Assertive communication is interacting and expressing yourself directly, positively, confidently, and with respect toward others, thus increasing the chances of being understood. It is being authentic about your thoughts and feelings.

Assertive communication can be contrasted with *aggressive communication* which is a hard charging approach, often carried out in a hostile manner, where the person comes across as controlling or dominating.

The three assertive communication skilled responses are: Describing; Stating Thoughts; and, Stating Feelings. We will discuss and practice each of these skilled responses in just a bit.

But first let us discuss "I" messages. *The "I" message is the cornerstone of assertive communication.*

The I message involves:

- Getting in touch with your observations, thoughts, and feelings regarding WIGO.

- Expressing those observations, thoughts, and feelings in an authentic manner.

The opposite of the I message is the "You message", which is the cornerstone of aggressive communication.

Figure 3.7: Contrasting "You messages" and "I messages"

"You message"		"I message"
Judgment or belief regarding what you said or did, or who you are.	**What It Is**	Your observation, thoughts, or feelings about what you said, did, or who you are and the impact on me.
Evaluating YOU.	**Focus**	Being authentic about ME. "Touching bases" with my thoughts and feelings.
"You didn't explain it very well."	**Example**	"I just don't get it."
Perceived as an attack.	**Likely Result**	Better chance of keeping the talk chain open, allowing any differences to be discussed.

In using the I message you acknowledge ownership of your reaction to WIGO and express yourself accordingly. This ownership of observations, thoughts, and feelings, and resultant expression (I message) most likely will make the other person less defensive than if you went out to the other person with a You message. The less the other person feels the need to go on defense, the more likely the both of you will be able to focus on any divergent viewpoints instead of each other.

The use of the I message does not necessarily mean that you will begin all your statements with "I", although that will generally be the case. For example, a statement such as: "The more we analyze, the more confusing things get for me", represents a genuine statement of frustration without using the word "I".

Conversely, just by using "I" does not necessarily make a statement an I message. For example, "I think your idea doesn't have any merit" most likely will be perceived as an attack, not an I message.

And don't think for a moment that there is anything soft about a skillfully expressed I message. It can be a powerful message. It does not take much skill to "clam up" (sullen silence); lash back (attack); or make a joke (deceiving). In fact, kids are great at natural responses. But it takes skill and some courage to be authentic about yourself.

A couple of *important guidelines* for you in becoming skillful in using I messages:

- **Be succinct.**

    Just "touch bases with yourself" in verbalizing your observations, thoughts or feelings. Do not go on at length. Nobody wants to listen to a five minute I message.

- **Go back and forth in a conversation about differences.**

    That is, "touch bases with yourself", and then go back to the other person with an Inquiry. For example: *"What are your thoughts about what I just said?"*. Or a Paraphrase/Speculate. For example: *"Based on your earlier comments, I'm thinking you may have some reservations about what I just said. Am I correct?"* [Speculate + Inquiry]). Pemberton coined such back-and forth-communication flow as "the conversational two step".

Due to the pivotal role the I message plays in assertive communication, it was advantageous to review the concept here before looking at each of the subset skills. Now let us turn to each of the assertive communication skilled responses.

ASSERTIVE COMMUNICATION: SKILLED RESPONSES

Describing

Describing is stating a topic or someone's statements or behaviors you want to talk about. When describing statements or behaviors, do so in observable and objective terms without interpreting or judging.

Some important thoughts regarding describing:

- Focus on the topic behavior, or action, not the person.
- Be direct and sincere.
- When context is needed, start with providing the context.

    For example:

    "I'd like to discuss the concern you raised yesterday in the staff meeting about the need to gain greater clarity relative to individual authorities."

> *"I noticed this week that in our two project meetings you did not share any ideas or provide any input."*

- If context is not needed, just go into your I message stating your thought or feeling. For example, *"I have sensed that your enthusiasm of late has waned."*

- When something happens in the moment you want to respond to, do so. For example, *"I need to stop you right there. I just don't see it that way."* Or, when you want to talk about something in general that does not focus on a specific statement or behavior. For example, *"I think we need to talk about our relationship."*

- After describing what you want to talk about or after stating a thought or feeling, most times it is useful to go back to the other person with a skilled response, that is, an inquiry or paraphrase/speculate. For example, using the statement above regarding your sensing a waning of enthusiasm, you could follow on with, if appropriate, an inquiry such, as: *"Am I right?"*. Or a speculation, such as: *"Is the assignment becoming too routine for you?"*

Stating Thoughts

Stating thoughts is exactly that. You are expressing your thinking and taking the responsibility regarding about how a situation, statement, or behavior affects you.

For example:
   "I find what has happened to be unclear and puzzling."
   "I think the new procedure is a big improvement."

Some important thoughts regarding stating thoughts:

- Use I messages, or "me" or "my" messages, to indicate that you own the thought.
- Express your thought in positive terms.
- As needed, constructively give reasons to explain the basis of your thoughts.

Stating Feelings

Stating feelings is expressing the emotion you feel about a situation, statement, or behavior.

As with stating thoughts, you are expressing the impact the situation, statement, or behavior has on you. The difference is that you are stating emotions. Thoughts are not emotions.

Some important thoughts regarding stating feelings;

- Describe the feeling you have, positive, negative, or neutral.

    For example:
    "I am annoyed."
    "I am delighted about the progress to date."

- State the feeling in sincere and constructive terms.

    For example:
    "I am angered when you do that" Not: *"I hate when you do that."*

- Focus on the situation, statement, or behavior, not the person.

- Link feelings to a description of a specific situation, statement, or behavior that triggered those feelings adds useful context.

For example:
"*Sam, when we disagree you often use an awful lot of profanity. (Describing) This bothers me (Stating Feelings). In fact, the profanity drowns out for me what you're disturbed about." (Stating Thoughts).*

Providing Constructive Feedback

The review of the assertive communication skills of describing, stating thoughts, and stating feelings, along with an understanding of The Ladder of Inference, makes it easy to recognize the difference between providing constructive feedback, positive or negative, and criticism or praise—an important distinction.

Constructive Feedback:	Stating *observations* regarding another person's specific behavior or actions and the impact of those behaviors or actions on you.
Praise:	Expressing a *favorable opinion* of what a person said or did, or who they are.
Criticism:	Expressing an *unfavorable opinion* of what another person said or did, or who they are.

Constructive feedback can be used for both positive and negative reinforcement. It works better than praise or criticism in wanting to see desirable behaviors or actions continued or undesirable behaviors or actions diminished or eliminated. The reason is that constructive feedback provides specific and timely information to the receiver rather than generalities.

ASSERTIVE COMMUNICATION SKILLS: PRACTICE

Exercise 3.3: Converting "You Messages" to "I Messages"

What to Do

1. Convert these "You messages" to "I messages". In doing so, as appropriate, describe the situation or behavior and its impact on you by stating a thought or feeling. You are going to have to ad lib a bit.
2. Compare your responses to those shown in Appendix A, "Questions and Answers", **Exercise, 3.3: Converting "I" Messages to "You" Messages**, pages 82, 83.

"You messages"

1. "You should stop talking that way."
2. "Your idea won't work."
3. "Why are you always too busy to talk to me when I call?"

Exercise 3.4: The New Safety Procedure

What to Do

1. Read the situation below.
2. Using the structure provided, state what you would say to Pete.
3. Compare what you would say to the response shown in Appendix A, "Questions and Answers", **Exercise, 3.4: The New Safety Procedure**, pages 83, 84.

The situation

A new safety procedure was recently implemented with your group. You told your staff about the importance of following this procedure in their work. You have noticed Pete does not use the procedure. In fact, earlier today you heard him say to a co-worker that he will not bother with the new procedure because it will only slow him down. This procedure is a requirement. You need to talk to Pete.

a. **Describe** what you want to talk to Pete about.
b. **State your thoughts** or **feelings** about the situation.
c. Reach out to Pete and get him involved in the conversation with an **inquiry** or a **paraphrase/speculate**.

KEEPING THINGS MOVING

Let us now discuss some of the ways you can optimize your conversations, especially your tough conversations, by assuring that they are fluid and move along. We have already discussed some of these pointers but they are included here as a matter of emphasis and a fuller explanation.

Remember the 3 R's of Effective Communications

Role: What's my role?
Am I a player here?
Is this really that important to me? What would happen if I left it alone?
Can I influence the situation?
What's the proper timing, and who should be involved?

Risk: Appreciate that effective communications when dealing with tough conversations is risky. It is risky because you never know what you are going to find as you are authentic about you and really trying to understand others.

Responsibility: I will clean up any messes I may create by using skillful communication patterns to reach out and/or be authentic.

Maintain a Growth Mindset

Your objective in communicating about differences should not be to win, convert, change, or even educate someone. You should go into such conversations with the objective of seeking to understand and to be understood. In such conversations the hope is that each party gain greater clarity regarding their respective mutual points of view. And perhaps have some learning and growth as well.

A reminder. The higher the level of the stage of awareness of the person you are attempting to communicate with is, in general or with respect to the specific topic, the easier it will normally be to have a respectful and constructive exchange. Dealing with a Stage II with an absolutistic or fixed mindset is normally tough sledding. This does not mean that you should not try. It is just going to be tougher than trying to communicate with a Stage III, Relativistic, or Stage IV, Transitory, person with a more growth-oriented mindset.

After being frustrated with trying to communicate about a difference with a fixed mindset, again regarding a specific topic or issue, or in general, the best thing is to avoid discussing the subject with that person, or if feasible, avoid the person. It is just not worth your time and effort. And he can be too toxic for you.

Be Present

We discussed the importance of attending and acknowledging the person you are attempting to communicate with as a precursor for active listening. That is, the importance of being present.

And you need to maintain this presence throughout your conversation. You need to focus on the person and her output channels (verbal, voice, and visual) in attempting to understand the real message. In doing so you need to forget about what you are going to say when it comes your turn. Doing so will only divert you from focusing on the other person and what she is trying to communicate. You will be surprised that when it comes your turn to talk that you have not missed a beat. In fact, you will be better off in responding because your understanding will be better.

Get a Rhythm Going

You can liken having an effective conversation to dancing. Even though you may not like the music that is being played, this analogy really holds up when you are engaged in difficult communications.

You want to try and establish a rhythm of going back and forth as you spin around the talk chain. Again, kind of a "conversational two step". Briefly out to you; then briefly back to me; then back to you; and so forth.

You can create such a rhythm through the use of skillful communication patterns. Inviting the other person in after your I message through inquiry or paraphrase/speculate. Using inquiry and paraphrase/speculate to help clarify and understand what they are saying before you talk.

And this is how you reap the benefits of the Principle of Reciprocity (or Caring) mentioned earlier.

> The Principle of
> Reciprocity (or Caring): *If you think I am trying to understand you, you may be indebted to try and understand me.*

This principle is huge in trying to understand and be understood. It paves the way for smooth transitioning.

Go to the Balcony

When engaged in strenuous efforts in attempting to communicate about differences, it is sometimes useful to imagine yourself, or yourselves, going up to the balcony and peering down on just what is happening. Not to lock in the words so much, but just to try and get an objective perspective or feel as to what kind of dance is going on.

The 3-Step Conflict Resolution model

There is the old adage that in conflict situations you have two alternatives—fight or flight. Sometimes one of these two alternatives may be appropriate.

But there is a third option. *"Can't we just talk about it and see if we can work things out?"*

The 3-Step Conflict Resolution Model is an invaluable model for communicating in conflict situations. Thank you, Bill Pemberton. It is easy to understand, but often not that easy to apply in uptight situations. But skillful communication patterns in conjunction with the model can make good things happen. Sometimes even magic.

Figure 3.8: The 3-Step Conflict Resolution Model

1. Seek to understand and be understood.
2. Seek to resolve ("What's possible?").
3. Agree on next steps.

TRANSITION

The purpose of this book is to give you an awareness and appreciation of communication patterns to help you constructively communicate about differences. Not only to gain an in-depth awareness, but also to encourage and enable you to hone your active listening and assertive communication skilled responses

Hopefully the book will continue to be a valuable reference and resource for you.

In any acquisition and use of knowledge and skills there are various levels of competence, as shown below.

Figure T1: Levels of Competence

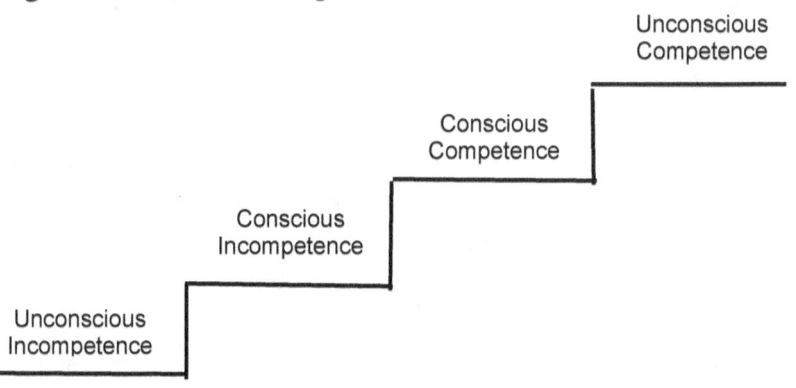

Unconscious Incompetence:	I don't even know that I lack the requisite knowledge or skill.
Conscious Incompetence:	I realize that I lack the requisite knowledge or skill.
Conscious Competence:	I am aware that I have some requisite knowledge or skill but need to keep working to improve.
Unconscious Competence:	I have mastered the knowledge or skill. But I must keep my knowledge up to date and my skill honed or they may diminish.

In speaking of levels of competence you are reminded of the analogy used earlier to make a useful distinction between ability and competence. Your ability in any particular area was likened to a bucket that has a fixed capacity. You can fill it up only so much. Your competence was likened to the liquid level inside the bucket. It represents your accumulated knowledge or skill in that particular area.

As you are working on gaining competence in a certain area you are striving to fill a particular ability bucket you have with knowledge or skill. The greater the degree of dedication, education and coaching, deliberate practice, and application, the greater your chances will be to accumulate knowledge and skill in that particular area. The size of your ability bucket in any particular area will dictate how far and how fast you will be able to progress up the various levels of competence.

Unfortunately, as discussed, the size of your ability bucket in any particular area will tend to get smaller as you age. The shrinkage typically occurs more rapidly and to a greater degree regarding physical abilities as compared to mental abilities. Injuries and illnesses are also factors in both kinds of abilities. Such is life.

Hopefully you will continue to work on enhancing your skillful communication patterns. Age should not be a factor.

Your attention is called to Appendix B, "Putting It to Work: Crafting Improvement Strategies", page 85. You will find a Development Plan Worksheet which is designed to help you plan and implement any specific improvements you want to work on.

APPENDIX A

ANSWERS AND COMMENTS

Chapter One

Exercise 1.1: Communications Barriers

Some verbal, voice, and visual barriers that can get in the way of communications:

- interrupting
- looking away
- fidgeting
- clamming up
- withdrawing
- getting defensive
- ridiculing
- going off on a tangent
- monotone
- referring to examples or events the other party doesn't share
- yelling
- attacking
- dismissing or making light of what the other party is saying
- making light of what is being said
- failing to make eye contact
- changing the subject before the other party has finished a thought
- too loud or low a tone of voice
- sarcasm
- insulting
- invalidating
- giving unsolicited advice
- being deceptive
- busy doing something else
- taking or making a phone call
- dragging on
- using words that the other party does not understand

Chapter Two

Exercise 2.1: What Do You See?

How about the first image to the left of the page. Do you see a goblet, or is that a fountain? Twins staring at one another? How do you know they are twins? See none of these images? See something else?

Over to the right, do you see what might be described as a young girl? An old lady? Both? Neither? Something else?

People tend to get particularly irked relative to this image for some reason if they do not see the young girl, the old lady, or both. The point relative to our discussion of perception is that it really doesn't matter. It's in the eye of the beholder.

But here goes, one time only. See if this helps. If not move on.

The young lady is looking over her right shoulder, with a feather in her dark hair. The old lady is looking down, with her chin tucked between what looks to be a fluffy coat or fur of some kind.

What about the final image? Do you see the face of what is commonly recognized as the face of Jesus Christ?

Exercise 2.2: Who Done It?

<u>Answers</u>

1. T
2. T
3. ?
4. T
5. ?
6. ?
7. ?
8. F
9. T

APPENDIX A: ANSWERS AND COMMENTS

Exercise 2.3: Deletion

There are 6 F's in the sentence. It is common for people to miss or *delete* the f's in the of's.

In using this exercise over the years in training sessions I have had answers that ranged from 2 to 8! Must have been the pressure.

EXERCISE 2.4: Distortion

If you said such things as: "I see a car parked at the curb;" "It is in front of a house with a Mr. Jones attached to it;" "There is a tree in the front yard"; and so forth, you stuck to the observation level.

If, however, in your description you said something like: "Dr. Smith is making a house call on Mr. Jones", you moved from the observation level in the Ladder of Inference and began ascending the rungs of the ladder going from sensing to postulating; from facts to assumptions. You began projecting yourself into the territory. And in so doing, increased the likelihood of *distortion* in your perception of what is going on.

For example: "How do you know Dr. Smith is a medical doctor?"; "If he is, he's making a house call, in today's world?"; "Are you sure someone is ill?" "Are you sure the car belongs to Dr. Smith?" You get the point.

As discussed earlier, there is nothing wrong with postulating and assuming things about what is going on. The purpose here is just to help you develop a greater level of awareness of when and to what degree you are making assumptions in your everyday mapmaking.

Exercise 3.1: Identifying the Most Useful Response

Statements

1. "I can't stand that new boss of mine. He's such an arrogant know-it-all. Everything that goes wrong he puts on me."

   a. "I guess all of us have a tough time breaking in a new boss."
   b. "Tell me what sort of things have been happening."

   The best response is b., which is an inquiry. You asked it because you thought it was relevant to help your understanding the speaker's issue. Response a. is a deceiving response making light of the speaker's concern, and thereby invalidating the concern.

2. "I'm really fed up with these reports. It looks like everything has to be done yesterday. Why can't we get a little more notice? There's no way to do a good job. What's so tough is that we spend a lot of time getting information that nobody is really going to use."

   a. "You find it hard to keep interested in doing a good job when you feel like you're under pressure to produce stuff that nobody uses."
   b. "You shouldn't feel that way. It's your job. And if something's not right, fix it."

   The best response is a., which incorporates both a paraphrase and a speculation. Response b. is a form of attack in that it both judging and advising relative to the speaker's statement.

3. "I'm running into some real problems with my group since I got promoted. It's hard to figure out how to relate to the people I used to work with, but now work for me."

   a. "How long have you had the new job?"
   b. "So, the relationship with the people you worked with has become strained since you became their boss."

These are both skilled responses and both would be appropriate depending on where you were at in your attempt to understand the speaker. Response a. is an inquiry which you would use to gain additional information which you think might be relevant to you in understanding the speaker's concern. Response b. is a paraphrase of the speaker's concern. You use it because you, unlike response a., think you have a clear enough picture to check out the speaker's meaning.

Exercise 3.2: Describe Appropriate Response

Statements

1. "I'm sorry I am late for our meeting again. I really tried to be on time, but I have a lot going on at home.

   Assuming you are somewhat taken back with the lateness, rather than giving a deceiving response like: "Well that's okay", it would probably be best to start with paraphrasing what was said about the cause of the lateness. Something like: "Lot going on the home front?" If the person wanted to elaborate you might allow a little bit of that, but then move quickly into the plan for the meeting. What you don't want to do is to be drawn into a long discussion regarding what is going on at home. Or, after paraphrasing, depending on how much you are upset, you might voice your concern about the importance of starting on time. (Assertive Communication)

2. You thought you had made your wishes clear. But then you are told the following:

   "I didn't know you wanted this done today. You never made that clear I thought we were going to talk about it in detail first."

   What you don't want to get started here is a blame game. A good start would probably be to paraphrase the situation. Something like: "Well it's obvious we had different interpretations about what was to be done and when". If appropriate, you might want to spend a little time to see what you could both learn from the situation, and how you could apply such learning in the future.

APPENDIX A: ANSWERS AND COMMENTS

3. You are about to start a meeting with a small group you have never met before, and you are hit with the following:

   "The last time we had one of these things nothing happened afterwards. All the things we agreed on were forgotten. These things are a waste of time."

   You might start out by acknowledging what was said. A paraphrase something like: "You are obviously upset about the lack of follow-on regarding similar meetings in the past". You then might want to inquire into the group to see to want degree the person's thoughts were shared. Assuming the thoughts are shared, you might want to inquire regarding suggestions for preventing a recurrence, and then go from there. Obviously, time will dictate as to how much detail you want or can get into in the moment. You will need to be sincere and commit to any recommendations you think are sound.

4. You come home from a hard day at work, and your spouse greets you with:

   "What a day I've had. The baby was crying all morning. The washing machine broke down, and I had to do things by hand. Then I went downtown to buy a hat and I had to wait 20 minutes for a bus. I couldn't find a thing I liked and everybody was so pushy and the store was so crowded. When I got back the baby sitter had the stew burnt—and I had worked so hard on it. I'm so mad I could cry. And I've got to go downtown again tomorrow."

   She probably doesn't want a string of inquiries regarding further details. And she certainly doesn't want to know about your hard day. At least not now. How about a slam dunk speculation like: "Wow, what a day from hell you've had!" After she let's you know that you've hit bullseye with something like: "You can say that again", you can give her a big hug. And perhaps inquire as to whether you fix her a drink.

Exercise 3.3: Converting "You Messages" to "I Messages"

There is no right answer here because we are not there in the situation and consequently do not know the dynamics. That is why you were encouraged to ad lib. Anyway, in so doing here are some I message responses that incorporate stating a thought, a feeling, and perhaps a description of the situation or statement.

1. You message: *"You should stop talking that way."*

    Possible I message: *"I get defensive and lose track of what you are trying to say when you come on so strong. I've been hesitant to bring it up, but thought it was important enough to talk about"*

    (Describing: *"Come on so strong"* + Stating Feelings: *"I get defensive"* (the impact of the behavior) and *"I've been "hesitant to bring it up..."* Stating Feeling.)

2. You message: *"Your idea won't work."*

    Possible I message: *"I have difficulty seeing how the idea will work."* (Stating Thought)

3. You message: *"Why are you always too busy to talk to me when I call?"*

    Possible I message: *"Whenever I've called lately you can't talk to me. And then I don't hear back. This bothers me and impedes my progress on the project."* (Describing Situation + Stating Feeling + Stating Thought regarding impact)

APPENDIX A: ANSWERS AND COMMENTS

As discussed in the chapter, instead of putting a period at the end of your I message it normally adds to the flow and makes for a more constructive conversation if you go back to the person with an inquiry or a paraphrase/speculate.

For example:

In the first I message an inquiry is not directly stated, but is implied by the *"I thought it was important enough to talk about."*

A logical inquiry for the second You message would be something like: *"Perhaps if I understood a little more of the rationale behind the idea it wouldn't be an issue for me."* Assuming that is what you really think.

For the third You message, *"Can we discuss?"* would seem to be an appropriate follow-on inquiry.

Exercise 3.4: The New Safety Procedure

The situation

A new safety procedure was recently implemented with your group. You told your staff about the importance of following this procedure in their work. You have noticed Pete does not use the procedure. In fact, earlier today you heard him say to a co-worker that he will not bother with the new procedure because it will only slow him down. This procedure is a requirement. You need to talk to Pete.

Again, in this exercise there is no right response. But the skilled talk pattern illustrated is useful to compare and contrast your response to what you would have said to Pete.

a. **Describe** what you want to talk to Pete about.
   "Pete, I noticed that you are not following the new safety procedure. I also heard that you don't intend to because it will slow you down."

b. **State your thoughts** and/or **feelings** about the situation.
   "I am greatly disturbed about your lack of compliance

c. Reach out to Pete and get him involved in the conversation with an **inquiry** or a **paraphrase/speculate**.
   "What the hell is going on?"

In going back to Pete, a good open-ended inquiry, as shown in c. above, is recommended rather than laying down the law early in the conversation. It is a good practice in such instances to give the person an opportunity to "explain away" the discrepancy. That is, to present their rationale for non-compliance. Again, we are not there so we don't have a feel for the serious of this discrepancy. But safety procedures are put into effect for a reason. After hearing Pete out, you may have some thoughts about making some modifications to the procedure. Or, you may need to give some heavy I messages to Pete stating that his behavior is unacceptable and he needs to be in strict compliance. And, if the violation was serious enough, along with his statements, assuming they are true, and putting that into the context of his record up to now, some form of disciplinary action may be in order.

APPENDIX B
PUTTING IT TO WORK: CRAFTING IMPROVEMENT STRATEGIES

Hopefully you have found the material covered in this book quite helpful and have begun using it in improving your communication effectiveness, especially when communicating about differences.

But some improvements you might want to make require a little bit more deliberate effort. That is what this appendix is about. To help you logically think through and implement specific communication behaviors you want to make.

In making a behavioral change of any significance the principle reviewed earlier and restated below is so critical to understand and use.

> *You are a product of the mental models you carry around and the practices you engage in. In other words, you are a product of your thoughts and behavior.*

The implications are when wanting to make any significant behavioral change you need to look at: a) mental models you may have to adopt or modify; and, b) practices that you need to engage in and monitor to transition to the desired behavior. In other words, you first need to review how you are thinking about the change. And then, to convert good intentions into action, what you specifically need to start doing or do more of, and stop doing or do less of, to successfully make the change.

You need to specifically think through:

- What is my specific goal? What is it that I am committed to achieve?
- What have I already tried? How did that go?
- What, if any, are the competing commitments[1] that stand in my way? These competing commitments may come in the form of mental models or habits that need to be modified of eliminated. Where did they come from, and how real are they?
- What additional knowledge or skills do I need?
- How do I know success when I see it? What are the specific evidences that will tell me that I have achieved the goal?
- What value will I derive by making this change?
- What are the specific practices I need to engage in to convert my good intentions into action?
- How am I going to gauge my progress?

Self-coaching is needed to convert your good intentions into action. Self-coaching comes in the form of practices and self-observation.[2]

Practices: Recurring behavior with a specific outcome or standard in mind.

The old adage that "practice makes perfect" is wrong. Practice makes permanent. What is needed is *deliberate practice.* That is, engaging in practices with a specific outcome or standard in mind. This important distinction applies to both mental models and habits you want to adopt, modify, or eliminate. Just practicing by itself without appropriate imaging may actually make matters worse. For example, in working on your golf game, I could go out and whack a gazillion golf balls on the practice range. But without the proper fundamentals in mind and a model to envision, you could become less competent in my ball striking prowess by grooving bad habits.

Self-observation: Specifying how you are going to monitor progress in achieving your goal. In golf you do this by seeing exactly what happens to the ball when you strike it on the practice range or out on the course. But you don't have practice ranges and actual games to compete in when making non-physical improvements, such as enhancing your effective talk patterns in handling conflict situations. That is where self-observation comes in. You need to construct your own methods of gauging progress. This is done by crafting appropriate questions for yourself to gauge just how well you are striking the ball.

An example:

You want to improve your contributions at your department staff meetings. You want to do a better job of thinking about when to speak up, what to say, and how to say it.

An appropriate practice: For the next two months at our weekly staff meetings, am going to keep the "3R's of Effective Communications" in mind and have them guide my communications. I am also going to have the active listening and assertive communication skillful responses be top of mind.

An appropriate resultant self-observation question: At the end of each meeting, ask myself: *"What did I say or do in today's meeting, if anything, that helped what was being discussed in the meeting?"*, and, *"What did I say or do in today's meeting, if anything, that hindered the discussion in the meeting?"*

Modify your practices and resultant self-observation questions and timeframe until you are satisfied with the level of conscious competence you reach. Maybe you even will reach the unconscious level of competence.

All of these important considerations in making any significant behavioral change are incorporated into the Development Plan Worksheet below.

Development Plan Worksheet

Opportunity or Challenge

Describe the situation or context of the goal you want to achieve.

Goal

What am I committed to achieve?

Past Attempts

What, if anything, have I already tried to help me achieve this goal? How well did these attempts go? What, if anything, does my analysis of these attempts tell me?

Competing Commitments

Are there any competing commitments that stand in the way of me achieving my goal? If so, what are they? Competing commitments most often are mental models or habits that need to be eliminated of diminished. Where did they come from? How real are they?

Enhanced Knowledge/ Skills

What knowledge or skills do I need to acquire of develop? How do I go about doing so?

Measures of Success

How do I know success when I see it? What are the evidences that I have achieved my goal?

Value

What value will I derive by achieving my goal?

Strategies for Moving Forward

What specifically am I going to do to achieve my goal?

Start with dealing with any competing commitments that may exist. What specifically are you going to do to eliminate them or reduce them as obstacles in achieving your goal?

List specific self-coaching strategies you will employ to achieve your goal.

- *What practices am I going to engage in the near future to move from good intentions to action?*
- *What self-observation questions am I going to ask myself to gauge my progress on my practices?*

Development Plan Worksheet

Example #1

Opportunity or Challenge

When I have something important to say I am often reluctant to speak up fearing I might offend someone or stir things up.

Goal

Be a lot more assertive in my communications so I can still be me but say what I want to say in important situations.

Competing Commitments

My nature is to hold back. So often in challenging situations I don' speak up and continue to hold on to the frustration associated with me not saying my piece.

Enhanced Knowledge/Skills

My current knowledge/skill level is adequate. I just need to deal with the Competing Commitments barrier.

Measures of Success

- My voice is being heard.
- I am using assertive communication, not aggressive communication.
- People are trying to understand me.
- People appreciate what I have to stay.
- My opinion is being asked for a lot more.

Value

- I feel better about myself.
- I can speak up and still be me.

Strategies for Moving Forward

In dealing with the competing commitment, I need to appreciate that good communications is risky as I open things up I need to deal with what I find. Assertive communication and active listening skills are the keys for me to move forward in speaking up.

Self-Coaching:

Practice: For the next month summarize in a journal at the end of each day:

- Any situations where I wanted to speak up but didn't. What stood in my way? If I had the opportunity to replay the situation, what would I say or do differently, if anything?
- Any situations where I normally would be hesitant to speak up, but did so.

Self-Observation:

- What did I say or do that was helpful?
- What did I specifically say in the way of assertive communication or active listening that was effective?
- Did I say or do anything that hindered communications?
- What did I learn?

Development Plan Worksheet

Example #2

<u>Opportunity or Challenge</u>

Based on constructive feedback and self-observation, I am determined to shift from a highly directive management style to one that, as situational variables justify, more collaborative and even delegative.

<u>Goal</u>

I am committed to be less directive and more collaborative and even delegative in my management style.

<u>Competing Commitments</u>

My nature to be in control and the influence of previous bosses has formed a mental model for me that I need to call the shots as a manager, especially on important matters. I fear that to do otherwise will be perceived as a sign of weakness.

<u>Enhanced Knowledge/Skills</u>

I can do it. Just need to deal with the Competing Commitment.

<u>Measures of Success</u>

- Greater staff involvement in decision-making.
- Better quality of decisions.

- Ease of implementation of decisions.

Value

- Accelerated and increased staff learning.
- Improved communication.
- Improved commitment.
- I am freed up to do higher level leadership and management work.

Strategies for Moving Forward

Implementation Guidelines:

- Share goal and rationale with my staff. Solicit their help in accomplishing the goal and any hopes and concerns they may have.
- Only share responsibilities and authorities when I am assured that people affected have the task-relevant maturity, that is, competence and motivation, to be successful.
- Provide an environment that continually encourages people to learn and grow and equip them with the appropriate tools and support to do so.

Self-Coaching:

Practices

Over the next two months:

- Keep a record of the decisions I make with staff that represent a shift in management style from what I would normally have done. Date each entry.

Include:

- o Any hopes and concerns I had when I used the collaborative or delegative style.
- o Any coaching I did to assure that affected staff members would be successful.

Self-Observation

For each summary I record, select an appropriate follow-up date and place in a follow-up file.

When each summary comes out of the follow-up file, reflect on:

- Results of the collaborative or delegative action.
- Any staff learning or growth.
- What I might have done differently.
- What I learned.

As appropriate, share what I learned with affected staff members.

ENDNOTES

Introduction
1. Carl Welte, *Making and Fulfilling Your Dreams as a Leader: A Practical Guide for Formulating and Executing Strategy, Second Edition.* The Ewings Publishing, 2022.
2. Carl Welte, *Building Commitment: Unleashing the Human Potential at Work, Second Edition.* The Ewings Publishing, 2022.

Chapter One
1. David Lapakko, *An Urban Legend Proliferates.* Published by Cornerstone: A Collection of Scholarly and Creative Works for Minnesota State University, Mankato, 2007.
2. Ron Crossland, *The Leader's Voice, Second Edition*, (New York, Select Books, Inc., 2008).
3. John Grinder and Richard Bandler, *The Structure of Magic II A Book about Communication and Change*, (Palo Alto, CA: Science and Behavior Books, Inc., 1976).
4. A good book for getting acquainted with the Myers-Briggs assessment model is:

   David Kersey and Marilyn Bates, *Please Understand Me: Character & Temperament Types*, (Del Mar, CA: Prometheus Nemesis Books, 1978).

   The book not only does a good job of explaining the four diametric types and the many types that are combinations of the four basic types, but also has a questionnaire for you to take and identify your type.

A good organizational and publishing resource is CPP: Consulting Psychologists Press, Inc. Palo Alto, California.

With regard to the DISC model and assessments, there are many purveyors. If you are interested in learning more about DISC, my recommendation is to go to www.assessments24x7.com.

Also, if interested, a book by the DISC leadership team is worth checking out: Brandon Parker, Jennifer Larson, and Tony Alexander, *What Makes Humans Tick: Exploring the Best Validated Assessments*, indie Books International, 2021.

Chapter Two
1. Alfred Korzybski, *Science and Sanity: An Introduction to Non-Arisotelian Systems and General Semantics*, Fourth Edition, (Englewood, NJ, Institute of General Semantics, 1958).
2. J. Samuel Bois, *The Art of Awareness*, (Dubuque, IA, 1966).
3. S.I. Hayakawa, *Language in Thought and Action,* Fifth Edition (Eugene, OR.: Harvest Original Publishing Company, 1991). Previous editions published by Houghton Mifflin Harcourt Publishing Company, Boston MA, 1941.
4. Dr. William H. Pemberton, *Sanity for Survival; A Semantic Approach to Conflict Resolution* (San Francisco, CA: Graphic Guides, Inc., 1991).
5. Pemberton, Ibid.
6. Gail E. Myers and Michele Tolela Myers, *The Dynamics of Human Communication: A Laboratory Approach*, Sixth Edition, (New York: McGraw-Hill Humanities/Socials Sciences/Languages, 1991).
7. Pemberton, op.cit.
8. Exercise from: "The Uncritical Inference Test", William Henry, International Society of General Semantics, San Francisco, CA.
9. Although I have modified the model, the term "Structure of Interpretation" comes from: James Flaherty, *Coaching: Evoking*

Excellence in Others, Fourth Edition, Butterworth Heineman, 1999.
10. Peter M. Senge, *The Fifth Discipline: The Art and Practice of the Learning Organization* (New York: Doubleday Currency, 1990).
11. Isabel Wilkerson, *Caste: The Origin of Our Discontents* (Random House: New York, 2020).
12. Ezra Klein, Why We're Polarized (New York: Avid Reader Press, 2020).
13. Daniel Goleman, *Emotional Intelligence: Why It Can Matter More than IQ* (New York: Bantam Books, 1995.).
14. Carol S. Dweck, Ph.D., *mindset: The New Psychology of Success: How We Can learn to Fulfill Our Potential,* (New York: Random House Publishing Group, 2007).
15. Pemberton, op.cit.
16. Added to model. Thomas A. Harris, MD, *I'm OK-You're OK* (New York: Harper Collins, 2004).
17. Korzbyski, op.cit.

Chapter Three

1. Doc Childre, *Freeze Frame: A Scientifically Proven Technique for Clear Decision Making and Improved Health* (Planetary Publications, 2nd Edition, 1998).
2. Bandler and Grinder entitled their two-volume work for clinicians a number of years back *The Structure of Magic.* The book covered some of the same material as this book but was much broader in scope. In this book the term is used in a much more specific way. That is, to refer to skilled talk responses.

Richard Bandler and John Grinder, *The Structure of Magic: A Book about Language and Therapy,* (Palo Alto, CA: Science and Behavior Books, Inc., 1975.

Richard Bandler and John Grinder, *The Structure of Magic II A Book about Communication and Change,* (Palo Alto, CA: Science and Behavior Books, Inc., 1976).

Appendix B
1. Robert Kegan and Lisa Laskow Lahey, *Immunity to Change: How to Overcome and Unlock the Potential in Yourself and Your Organization*, (Boston, Massachusetts, Harvard Business, 2009).
2. James Flaherty, op.cit.

ABOUT THE AUTHOR

Carl Welte founded Welte Associates in 1993. Welte Associates enables organizational leaders and teams to achieve desired business results by helping them build the organizational capabilities to do so. That is, the requisite strategy, structure, systems, and workforce capability to succeed.

His more than fifty years of organizational, management, and consulting experience has equipped him with the requisite wisdom and coaching skills to enable leaders and teams to effectively address their organization's opportunities and challenges.

He has held senior-level positions in both large and small organizations. Carl has also held leadership positions in a variety of professional, industrial, and educational associations.

Carl was a visiting faculty member for 12 years at the University of Idaho, teaching in its executive development program. He has also taught leadership and management programs in the University of California's extension learning system for more than 10 years.

He is the author of *Making and Fulfilling Your Dreams as a Leader: A Practical Guide for Formulating and Executing Strategy,* Second Edition, The Ewings Publishing, 2022; *Building Commitment: A Leader's Guide to Unleashing the Human Potential at Work,* Second Edition, The Ewings Publishing, 2022; and, *Communicating about Differences: Understanding, Appreciating, and Talking about Divergent Points of View,* Second Edition, The Ewings Publishing, 2022.

He has an MBA from the University of California, Berkeley, and a BS degree in business administration from the University of California.

Carl lives in Novato, CA with his wife Dee. They have three children, six Grandchildren, and one great grandchild.

He can be reached at:

>Welte Associates
>14 Plata Court
>Novato, CA 94947
>Phone: (415) 328-1349
>Email: carl@welte.com
>Website: welte.com

www.ingramcontent.com/pod-product-compliance
Lightning Source LLC
LaVergne TN
LVHW092053060526
838201LV00047B/1374